Living in difficult times ...

by Ken Wooldridge

ISBN: 0979022045
ISBN-13: 9780979022043

Author and Publisher:
Ken Wooldridge
P.O. Box 7312,
Knoxville, TN 37921, USA
www.kenwooldridge.org

Cover design – Michael Dutton
Printed by CreateSpace in the USA
First printing 2013

Difficult times are ahead!

I have considered and reflected on the following:
- World political events that are happening
- A world economical crises that is immanent
- The fulfillment of Bible Prophecies
With that in mind it seems inevitable that we will need to know how to live in difficult times.

**In Gods creative genius He made provision
for man in nature!**

Genesis 1:11-12, 29
"And God said, behold, I have given you every herb bearing seed, which is upon the face of all the earth, and every tree, in the which is the fruit of a tree yielding seed; to you it shall be for meat."

Psalm 104:14.
"God ... causeth the grass to grow for the cattle
and herb for the service of man."

About the author

Ken Wooldridge was born in Botswana and raised in Africa.
He has been living in Tennessee for over twenty years.
He has learned and enjoyed the benefits of foraging wild plants.
This book contains a vast amount of valuable information he
has compiled.
The purpose of this book is to help you and those you love.

Disclaimer

Read this disclaimer before reading this book.
Information presented herein is intended for your reading pleasure and educational purposes only.
It is not the intention of the author to advise on health issues.
Please see a medical professional about any health concerns you have.
Statements in this book have not been evaluated by the FDA.
Before using any of this information, it is always advisable to consult with your Doctor or Healthcare Provider first.
When undergoing any medical treatment or procedures, readers or those they are advising, should consult their medical practitioners before making decisions about their medical prescriptions and treatments.
If any information provided herein is used, individual results and reactions may vary from person to person.
Those who are experiencing allergies should consult their medical practitioners before making decisions about their medical prescriptions and treatments.
Readers are advised to research other sources also, to compare with information in this book.
The author and publisher make no warranties, expressed or implied, regarding the accuracy of the material provided in this book.
The author and publisher assume no legal or other liability, or responsibility for any loss or injuries that may result from the use of information contained in this book.

Reading and using information in this book will constitute your acceptance of this disclaimer.

Contents

Chapter One:
What is needed in difficult times?

There are at least ten things that are needed:

1. An emergency fund.

1. If you are unable to access your bank account when adverse circumstances arise, cash saved in a secure place will be a lifesaver.
It may be used for things such as food, clothes, fuel, medicine and transportation.
(If possible have at least $2000.00 cash stashed away for such emergencies.)

2. Be prepared for eight possible Disasters that may occur without warning:

1. An Earthquake
2. A Tornado
3. Flooding
4. Fire
5. An Epidemic
6. Biological contamination.
7. Nuclear contamination
8. An economic Depression

3. Knowledge of emergency evacuation routes:

In the case of a sudden disaster occurring, immediate evacuations are often required.

Have a clear knowledge of all evacuation routes, in all directions from where you are.

Choose and notate the major routes you may use when travelling:

North

....

South

....

East

....

West

....

All family members need to ensure who their phone contacts are outside of their State in all directions.

Once they have evacuated, they will need to contact these contacts by phone, to advise them of where they are and how they are doing.

These contacts will in turn contact your family and close friends to help them re-unite with you after the evacuation is over.

North
Name: .... Phone: ..../........./............

South
Name: .... Phone: ..../........./............

East
Name: .... Phone: ..../........./............

West
Name: ...., Phone: ..../........./.............

4. Communications:
It is advisable to create a specific and easy communication system between;
- Local family members
- Distant family members
- Friends

Be sure to have mobile phones and chargers wherever you go.

5. Media communications:
It is advisable to be able to receive news reports from;
- Local and national Radio & TV stations (Possibly by battery operated receivers)
- A two-way radio or Ham radio

6. Transportation:
To maintain transportation during difficult times, the following may be needed;
- Emergency Gasoline for a vehicle
- A suitable vehicle for transportation
- Road maps
- Possibly a four wheel drive vehicle or Dirt bike

7. Accommodation and equipment:
For living and sleeping -
Tent
Sleeping bags
Inflatable mattresses
Candles
Flashlights
Batteries
Portable Potty
Portable Shower
Survival Blankets

Living in Difficult Times

For cooking and heat -
Methanol Gel heaters for food
Lighters and matches
Fire starting equipment
Gas cookers and heaters
Propane Gas
Wood
Grill (wood or propane)
Cooking utensils
Plates, cups, knives, forks and spoons

Other-
Battery Radio
Walky-talky
Survival book
Multi tool
Water purifying tablets or drops
Lighter, metal match or waterproof matches
Compass
Fish snare line and fishhooks
Needle and thread
Knife
Fire extinguisher
Gas masks

When an area is placed in quarantine you will need:
Clear plastic to seal windows and doors of your home or
    vehicle
Masking tape

8. Emergency food and necessities:
(At least a 6 month supply of food, adjusted to your family
needs)
A suggestion of any of the following:
Water – for drinking and washing
Coffee
Tea
Sugar

Salt
Spices
Powder soft drink
Powder milk
Rice
Cornmeal
Flour
Bisquick
Macaroni
Spaghetti
Cooking oil
Vinegar
Crackers
Cookies
Peanut Butter
Jelly
Gravy mix
Ketchup
Mustard
Cereal
Cheese
Chips
Snacks
Other -

Canned -
Baked beans
Pinto beans
Green beans
Peas
Tomatoes
Potatoes
Yams
Beets
Chilli
Ragu
Sweet Corn
Mixed Vegetables
Tuna
Soup

Living in Difficult Times

Mixed Fruit
Garlic
Beef
Chicken
Weenies
Beef and vegetable broth
Beef or chicken cubes
Other -

Fresh fruits and vegetables – always stored in a cool place
Apples / Oranges / Potatoes/ Cabbage / Carrots / Dry beans
  / Onions

Toiletries
Toothpaste
Soap
Shampoo
Deodorant
Laundry detergent
Toilet rolls
Shaving equipment
Other -

Medications -
Anti-biotic
Nyquil
Vicks-rub
Nasal spray
Chloroseptic throat spray
Imodium
Pepto-Bismol
Cortisone for skin allergies
Salve for cuts and bruises
Hydrogen Peroxide solution – as an external antiseptic
Other -

9. Emergency equipment
Survival kit -
> First Aid Kit
> Basic Emergency Supplies
> Bandages and adhesive strips
> Gauze pads
> Alcohol pads
> Antiseptic pads
> Moleskin
> Travel towels
> Steel needles
> Stainless-steel scissors
> Emergency blanket
> Emergency poncho
> Signal whistle
> Iodine tablets
> Waterproof matches
> Glow sticks
> Other -

10. Organic Seeds
From your local Famers Co-Op
Websites of online suppliers:
www.harrisseeds.com/Storefront/s-133-organic-vegetable-seed.aspx
www.gardenharvestsupply.com/productcart/pc/Organic-Vegetable-Seeds-c237.htm
www.heirloom-organics.com/or/organicvegetableseeds.html
www.seeds-organic.com/
www.mainstreetseedandsupply.com/Organic_Seed_s/59.htm
www.ufseeds.com/Organic-Vegetable-Seeds.html
or
Google search online for other suppliers.

11. Books and material
For more information you may find the following of value:
> - The Complete Wilderness Training by Hugh Mc Manners
> - Boy Scout Handbook and Field book

Notes
Additional things needed

Chapter Two:
What to do when a crisis arises

It is important to be fully prepared for any kind of crisis that arises.
As previously stated, there are at least eight possible crises situations:

1. An Earthquake
2. A Tornado
3. Flooding
4. Fire
5. An Epidemic
6. Biological contamination
7. Nuclear contamination
8. An economic Depression

In any such crises you should know how to immediately react
You should:

1. Understand what and how serious the situation is
2. Overcome the immediate surprise, shock and calm yourself
3. Assess damage or hurts experienced and prepare for pending or imminent danger
4. Maintain your composure and calm your family
5. Visualize your plan to protect yourself and those you love
6. Immediately implement your plan to deal with the situation
7. Delegate responsibilities to all involved
8. Complete the plan dealing with the situation

Living in Difficult Times

Websites you may choose to visit:
http://www.fema.gov/plan/index.shtm
http://www.72hours.org/
http://www.prepare.org/
http://theepicenter.com/howto.html

Survival Management
During any crises, discipline is of utmost importance.
Create and implement a survival management plan.

It may consist of the following:
A daily activity program during the crises -
    Wake up time
    Bathroom times and personal Hygiene
    Making beds and clean up
    Devotions
    Breakfast
    Special tasks
    Lunch
    Relaxation
    Special tasks
    Dinner
    Listening to News Broadcasts for updated information
    Devotions
    Relaxation
    Sleep

Meal preparation
    Menu
    Food locations
    Those doing the cooking and clean up

Other
    Stock control
    Inventory of food on hand

Where and how to find extra food required
A continued replacement of required food and necessities

Sources of food supply

Vegetable garden
Meat locations
Foraging
Fishing
Hunting
Vegetable and fruit locations
Hand outs
Bartering

Sources of other supplies

Gasoline
Propane
Medications
Animal Feed
Vegetable seeds

Management

Finances
Workers
Daily program
Bathroom times
Work responsibilities
Discipline and order
Handling disputes

Supply line

Drivers
Vehicles
Gas locations
Maintenance of vehicles

Medical information and prescriptions
For those receiving medical treatments

Medical Doctor:

.... Phone: ....

Dentist:

.... Phone: ....

Pharmacist:

.... Phone: ....

Chapter Three:
Different wild plants
foraged for food

Vegetable similarities or substitutes:
Like tomatoes -
Autumn Olive berries
Ground Cherries (Husk Tomatoes) to be eaten only when ripe
Like carrots and turnips-
Queen Anne's lace root – slight bitter taste
Like cucumber -
Indian cucumber root
Cattail young inner stalks
Like celery -
Sochan young stems
Like beets -
Evening primrose roots
Like beans -
Squash tendrils
Sweet pea tendrils
Cucumber tendrils
Grape Vine tendrils
Sponge gourd tendrils
Green Brier tendrils
Reed grass – young stems cut and steamed
Like Broccoli -
Wild Mustard flower buds and young seedpods (springtime)
Milkweed flower buds –
(Unopened buds are delicious. Put them in a pot, pour on boiling water, boil one minute and drain. Repeat this process

three times or until no bitterness remains. Cook them a little longer until tender and serve with butter. They have a musky flavour.

Like Turnips -
Evening Primrose taproots
(Peel and boil the pale pink, first year taproot for up to 30 minutes, in two or three changes of water and serve with butter. It is mildly pungent but excellent.
They become milder during late fall, or early spring.)

Like Asparagus -
Cattail centres
Daylily new shoots
Poke young shoots
Solomon seal young shoots

Like cabbage -
Cattail young shoots

Like corn on cob -
Cattail young green flowers boiled, buttered and served like corn on the cob.
(They will become brown in summer)

Like potatoes -
Jerusalem artichoke tubers
Arrowhead tubers

Salads
Salad leaves –
   Wild mustard greens (early spring)
   Young Amaranth
   Young lambs quarters
   Young Solomon seal
   Evening primrose
   Dandelion leaves in spring and flowers (slightly bitter)
   Mullein – flowers are sweet (high in nutrition)
   Wild lettuce
   Broad leaf plantain
   Shepherds purse
   Chickweed
   Clover
   Watercress
   Blue violet

Sorrel
Henbit
Sassafras
Sorrel
Purslane leaves and stems, chopped

Salad additions -
Wild edible Mushrooms
Jerusalem artichoke root - thin slices
Cattail centres – thin slices
Wild onions
Ramps
Green brier tendrils
Orange/yellow Daylily flower petals
Rose, Yucca and Honeysuckle flower petals
Yucca flowers (Centres removed) arranged on top of salad
Nuts
and
(Like celery)
- Sochan young stems
(Like cucumbers or zucchini in thin slices)
- Bamboo centres
- Indian cucumber root
- Cattail stalks harvested early
(Like carrots)
- Queen Anne lace roots – slight bitter taste

Wild edible Mushrooms
Puff ball
Morel
Wine cap
Prince
Dryad saddle
Oyster
Bolette
Chanterelle
Chicken of woods
Horse
Meadow
Many other varieties

Living in Difficult Times

Greens
Amaranth
Chickweed
Dandelion
Mullein
Poke
Sheep sorrel
Ramps
Sochan
Curled dock
Lambs quarters
Mustard greens
Watercress

Nuts
Walnut
Pecan
Hickory
Acorn
Beechnut

Fruit
Pawpaw
Persimmon
Passion vine
Wild cherry
Muscadine
Bunch berry
Blackberry
Blueberry
Raspberry
Mulberry
Possum grapes
Wild strawberry
Prickly pears

Drinks
Lemonade made from:
> Dandelion flowers
> Wood sorrel leaves
> Kudzu flowers (pink)
> Elderberries
> Sumac berries

> *Tea made from:*
> Elderberry
> Sassafras
> Sweet birch
> Yarrow
> Mullein (builds the immune system)
> Spice bush
> Goldenrod leaves and flowers

> *Coffey made from:*
> Chicory root (baked and ground)
> Dandelion roots (baked and ground)
> A combination of Chicory, dandelion and beet roots (baked and ground)

Gelatine made from:
> Green Brier knobby roots – (ground and added to the ingredients and then cooked)

Soup thickener (ground)
> Day lily flowers
> Cattail roots (clean very well)
> Dried sassafras leaves
> Kudzu roots

Meats (See State Law for the fishing and hunting season)

Wild turkey
Rabbit
Wild Boar
Deer
Fish
Bird
Turtle
Squirrel

Chapter Four:
Wild edible plant times

March – September

There are many edible plants that may be foraged or foods used in this season.

They should be thoroughly cleaned before usage:

Soup
Dandelion
Wild onion
Mushroom
Amaranth
Sheep sorrel
Stinging nettle
Bean
Vegetable
Chicken noodle

Dryad saddle
Oyster
Bolette
Chanterelle
Chicken of
woods
Puff ball
Horse
Meadow
Puff ball

Soup
thickener
(ground)
Cattail roots
Kudzu roots

Mushrooms
Morel
Wine cap
Prince

Drinks
Lemonade:
Dandelion
flowers
Wood sorrel
leaves
Elderberries
Sumac berries

Salad
Dandelion
leaves
Chickweed
Clover leaves
Watercress
Purslane leaves
Sheep sorrel
leaves
Plantain leaves
Curled dock
leaves
Sassafras
leaves
Creeping
cucumber
Sorrel

Fruit
Pawpaw
Persimmon

Passion vine
Wild cherry
Muscadine
Bunch berry
Possum grape
Prickly pear
Seasoning
Truffles

Seed
Sprouting
(Sprout and use
as a vegetable)
Wheat / Beans /
Peas / Lentils /
Corn
Other

Tea leaves
Goldenrod
Plantain

Living in Difficult Times

Sassafras root

Greens
Amaranth leaves
Chickweed leaves
Dandelion leaves
Mullein leaves
Sheep sorrel leaves
Sochan leaves
Curled dock leaves
Ramps
Cactus leaves

Meat
(see State Law for the hunting season)
Wild turkey
Fish
Bird

Deer
Wild Boar
Rabbit
Turtle
Squirrel

Gravy-thickener
(ground)
Day lily flowers
Sassafras leaves
Cattail roots
Kudzu roots

Coffey
Dandelion roots
Beet roots
Chicory roots

Bird eggs

Vegetables
Wild Asparagus
Cattail heart
Milkweed

Green Brier Tendrils
Wild garlic & onions
Cattail shoots
Bamboo shoots
(Roots – like Potato)
Jerusalem Artichoke
Orange/Yellow Daylily
Arrow head
(Roots – like Beets)
Evening Primrose
(Celery)
Sochan stems
(Like Carrots)
Queen Anne lace
(like - string beans)
Unopen daylily buds

(Broccoli)
Milkweed flower buds
Wild mustard flower buds
(like
– Tomato's)
Olive berries-when ripe
(Wild Mushrooms)
Puff ball
Morel
Wine cap
Prince
Dryad saddle
Oyster

Gelatin
(Ground)
Green Brier knobby roots

October – November

There are many edible plants that may be foraged or foods used in this season.

They should be thoroughly cleaned before usage:

Soup
Dandelion soup
Cream of wild onions
Cream of Mushrooms
Chicken noodle
Amaranth soup
Sheep sorrel
Stinging nettle soup
Bean soup
Vegetable soup

Gravy-thickener
(ground)
Day lily flowers
Cattail roots
Sassafras leaves

Drinks
Lemonade:
Dandelion flowers
Wood sorrel leaves
Kudzu flowers
Elderberry berries
Sumac berries
Tea leaves
Elderberry
Sassafras
Sweet birch
Yarrow

Mullein
Spice bush
lance leaf goldenrod
Plantain

Coffey
Chicory roots
Dandelion roots

Salad
Dandelion leaves
Chickweed leaves
Clover leaves
Watercress leaves
Purslane leaves
Blue violet leaves
Wild lettuce leaves
Sheep sorrel leaves
Wood sorrel leaves
Henbit leaves
Plantain leaves
Shepherds purse leaves
Curled dock leaves
Sassafras leaves
Yucca flowers
Lambs quarters leaves

Creeping cucumbers

Fruit
Paw-paw
Persimmon
Passion vine
Wild cherry
Muscadine
Bunch berry
Mulberry
Plantain
Passion flower
Fox grape
Possum grape
Prickly pear

Seasoning
Truffles

Greens
Amaranth leaves
Chickweed leaves
Dandelion leaves
Mullein leaves
Poke leaves
Sheep sorrel leaves
Sochan leaves
Curled dock leaves
Lambs quarters leaves
Stinging nettle leaves

Evening Primrose leaves
Ramps
Cactus

Meat (see State Law for hunting season)
Wild turkey
Rabbit
Fish
Bird
Deer
Wild Boar

Gelatin
(ground)
Green Brier knobby roots

Nuts
Walnut
Pecan
Hickory
Acorn
Beechnut

Vegetables
Wild Asparagus
Cattail heart
Milkweed
Green Brier Tendrils
Wild garlic & onions
Cattail shoots

Living in Difficult Times

Bamboo shoots
(Roots – like Potato)
Jerusalem Artichoke
Orange/Yellow Daylily
Arrow head
(Roots – like Beets)

Evening Primrose roots
(Like Celery)
Sochan stems
(Like Carrots)
Queen Anne lace roots
(Like Broccoli)

Milkweed flower buds
Wild mustard flower buds

Flour
(Ground)
Honey locust pods
Nuts

Green brier roots
Pigweed seed
Yellow dock seed
Cattail pollen

Wild Mushrooms
Oyster

December – February

There are many edible plants that may be foraged or foods used in this season.

They should be thoroughly cleaned before usage:

Soup
Wild onion
Mushroom
Chicken
Bean soup

Greens
Lambs quarters
Collard greens
Curled Dock
Chickweed

Indoor vegetables

Stored vegetables

Bird
Deer
Wild Boar
Rabbit
Turtle
Squirrel

Gravy or soup thickener
(ground)
Cattail roots
Kudzu roots
Slippery elm root
Sassafras leaves

Indoor Seed Sprouting
(Sprout and use as a vegetable)
Wheat / Beans
Peas / Lentils
Corn

Coffey
Chicory roots

Meat
(see State Law for hunting season)
Wild turkey
Fish

Bird eggs

Notes
Wild edible plant times

Chapter Five:
What, when and where to forage wild edible plants

Five basic foraging rules:

1. Never forage or eat anything you cannot positively identify as safe
2. Never pick endangered plant species
3. Always protect plants and nature
4. Only pick as much as you need and never take all the plants where you forage
   (This will give them time to recover and multiply.
   By doing that, you will be able to return back and forage again next season)
5. At all times be careful of poisonous plants, snakes and insects.
   (A helpful website is - http://www.wilderness-survival. net/snake/1/)
6. Only forage in unrestricted areas or obtain permission from a landowner to forage.

Many of these herbs, plants, shrubs and trees may be found growing where you are, or in surrounding areas.

For Wild Plant Pictures go to my website -
www.kenwooldridge.org - go to - *foraging wild plants*
Pictures are always updated and new ones are added from time to time.

Amaranth - Amaranthus
- Habitat: roadsides, vacant lots and fields
- Height: 3 to 6 ft
- Leaves: can be green or red, depending on the variety
- Time: spring to summer for the leaves and summer or fall for seeds
- Use: tender young leaves in salads or cooked like spinach. Leaves dried and crushed to a fine powder may be used in soups, gravy and jelly.
- Cooking time: Simmer amaranth in water for 12-15 minutes
- Seed: eaten raw or ground into flour
- Nutritional value: This food is low in Saturated Fat, and very low in Cholesterol. It is also a good source of Niacin, Protein, Vitamin A, Vitamin C, Riboflavin, Vitamin B6, Folate, Calcium, Iron, Magnesium, Phosphorus, Potassium, Zinc, Copper and Manganese.

Arrowhead tubers - Sagittaria latifolia
- Habitat: shallow water or wet soil at the edge of streams, ponds and marshes
- Height: 1-4 feet
- Leaves: have an arrow shape and veins from the centre
- Flowers: are white
- Time: Blooms June through October
- Use: Tubers are cooked like potatoes or sliced and used in a stir fry
- Nutritional value: Source of starch.

Autumn olive berries - Elaegnus umbellate
- Habitat: found on bushes along roads and streams
- Height: a large shrub or small tree
- Leaves: silver green leaves
- Flower: fragrant, ivory-yellow flowers
- Fruit: resembles a small cranberry
- Time: fall
- Use: used like tomatoes or for jam and jelly
- Nutritional value: vitamins A, C, E, flavonoids, essential fatty acids and lycopene.

Bamboo
- Habitat: very selective areas
- Height: up to 20 ft
- Time: most of the year
- Use: Young shoots may be used in soups and with stews Centres may be sliced in Chinese stir fry dishes
- Nutritional value: is low in Saturated Fat, and very low in Cholesterol. It is also a good source of Dietary Fibre, Protein, Riboflavin, Zinc, Vitamin B6, Potassium, Copper and Manganese.

Bear Corn - Conopholis Americana
- Habitat: Found on the roots of woody plants, especially oaks and beech trees
- Height: It is cone-shaped and 4 to 8 inches
- Flowers: It has close yellow/cream flowers all around the stem with a swollen base, facing down. They becomes brown throughout the summer and shrivelled and black in winter
- Time: Found above ground in spring
- Use: may be prepared and eaten as corn on the cob.

Blue violet - Viola odorata
- Habitat: on lawns, woods, meadows, waste areas and along rivers
- Height: 3-8 inches tall
- Leaves: heart-shaped leaves up to 3 inches long
- Flowers: blue-purple up to 1 inch
- Time: spring through summer
- Use: flowers and young leaves can be added to salads and has a slight bland taste
- Nutritional value: contains antioxidants.

Burdock - Arctium lappa
- Habitat: roadsides, vacant lots and fields
- Height: 2-9 feet tall
- Leaves: large elephant like leaves that are white and fuzzy underneath
- Time: spring to late fall

- Use: roots are like potatoes
- Cooking time: scrub / scour and simmer for 20 minutes like potatoes
- Nutritional value: contains valuable minerals such as iron, manganese, magnesium and small amounts of zinc, calcium, selenium, and phosphorus.

Cactus
- Habitat: sunny fields or on mountain sides
- Height: up to 8 ft
- Leaves: are like pads available all year - younger pads are tastier
- Use: peeled pads can be eaten raw, pickled, fried or made into jerky
- Nutritional value: Contains vitamins A, B6, C, calcium, magnesium, sodium, niacin, iron, folate, phosphorus and zinc. (Be careful of the tiny thorns)

Cattail - Typha latifolia
- Habitat: wet soil at the edges of streams, ponds and marshes
- Height: up to 8ft and the tops look like the tail of a cat that turn brown in summer
- Leaves: Long stalks
- Time: Spring though summer
- Use: roots ground to flour or used as sauce or a gravy thickener The heart of the stalk is used like asparagus
- Nutritional value: a source of starch

Chamomile
- Habitat: It is a low growing garden plant
- Height: about 12 inches high
- Leaves: They are divided into fine thread-like segments with a feathery appearance
- Flower: A daisy like flower with white florets and a yellow centre
- Time: July through September

- Use: Flower heads are ground and used for a tea for stomach problems, colds, muscle -aches, anxiety and insomnia
- Nutritional value: contains carbohydrates, calcium, magnesium, potassium, fluoride, folate and vitamin A.

Chicory – Cichorium intybus
- Habitat: roadsides, vacant lots and fields
- Height: up to 4 ft tall
- Flowers: dark sky blue colour
- Time: spring through fall
- Use: taproot roasted and ground for coffee
- Nutritional value: is low in Saturated Fat and Cholesterol. A good source of Thiamin, Niacin, Zinc, Vitamins A, B6, C, E, K, Riboflavin, Folate, Pantothenic Acid, Calcium, Iron, Magnesium, Phosphorus, Potassium, Copper and Manganese

Chickweed - Stellaria media
- Habitat: lawns and in open, sunny areas, as well as partially shaded areas
- Height: forms mats and stalks are about 8 inches long
- Leaves: tiny, pointed, oval, un-toothed leaves
- Flower colour: white flowers about 1/8 inch with 5 petals
- Time: all year
- Use: cook like spinach
- Cooking time: 5 minutes
- Nutritional value: Rich in iron, potassium, vitamins A, B, C, D and minerals.

Clover - red - Trifolium pratense
- Habitat: in meadows and on lawns
- Height: about 12 inches
- Leaves: Has a 3 leaf grouping
- Flower colour: red **(do not use white flower clover)**
- Time: spring
- Use: flowers make a good herb tea or used raw with the young leaves in salads

- Nutritional value: it contains calcium, chromium, magnesium, niacin, phosphorus, potassium, thiamine, vitamin A, B-complex, C, zinc, iron, selenium, cobalt, nickel, manganese, tin and sodium.

Curled dock - Rumex Crispus
- Habitat: roadsides, vacant lots and fields
- Height: 1 to 5ft
- Leaves: wavy long, lance-shaped, hairless leaves
- Flower: green flowers that become clusters of hard, reddish fruit
- Time: Spring and summer
- Use: nutritious, lemon flavoured young leaves, raw or cooked in early spring
- Cooking time: simmer for 5 minutes
- Nutritional value: leaves are rich in vitamins A, C and minerals especially iron.

Warning - they contain chrysophanic acid that can irritate or numb your tongue.

Dandelion - Taraxacum officinalis
- Habitat: lawns, roadsides, vacant lots, and fields
- Height: 2" to 18" tall
- Leaves: long, lance-shaped toothed leaves
- Flower colour: yellow flowers are 1 to 2 inches wide
- Time: spring to fall
- Use: salads and stir fries (including flowers) – roots roasted and ground for coffee
- Nutritional value: contains vitamins A, B1, B2, B3, C, D, E, Boron, Calcium, Chromium, Copper, Cobalt, Iron, Magnesium, Manganese, Molybdenum, Phosphorus, Potassium, Sodium, Selenium, Silicon and Zinc.

Daylily - Hemerocallis fulva
- Habitat: gardens or fields
- Height: up to 4ft high
- Flower colour: orange or yellow petals
- Time: Use shoots in spring, flower buds and flowers from spring to summer

- Use: raw shoots and flowers used in salads, sautéed, stir-fried or simmered in soups.
  Unopened buds can be cooked like string beans
- Nutritional value: contains Calcium, Phosphorus, Iron, Sodium, Potassium, Vitamins A, C, Thiamin, Riboflavin and Niacin.

Elderberry - Sambucus canadensis
- Habitat: on roadsides, in moist woods, in marshes and along riverbanks
- Height: up to 13 ft
- Leaves: oval leaflets with pointed tips
- Flowers: white, flat rounded clusters of lacy flowers 6 inches across
- Time: late spring and summer
- Fruit: juicy purple berries replace the flowers, ripening from mid-summer to fall
- Use: sauté the flowers or make fritters, mixing them with pancake batter
  The ripe purple berries can be used in muffins, cakes and breads
- Nutritional value: high in vitamins A, C, B6, iron and is a powerful antioxidant that is high in fibre.

Evening primrose - Oenothera biennis
- Habitat: fields, sunny woods, waste ground and road sides
- Height: 4 to 5 ft
- Leaves: Alternate lemon scented hairy lance-like leaves, 3 to 6 inches long
- Flower: 2½ inches in diameter, bright yellow and has four cross shaped petals
- Time: June to September
- Use: leaves cooked as greens, the flowers added to salads and the roots boiled like beets or turnips
- Nutritional value: the seed is rich in linoleic acid which is good for optimal health.

Goldenrod - Solidago lancifolia
- Habitat: roadsides, vacant lots and fields
- Height: up to 5 feet
- Leaves: have serrated leaf margins
- Flowers: have small yellow flowers clustered in panicles, forming a lance like shape
- Time: they bloom in late summer and fall
- Use: tea made from the leaves and flowers is used for sore throat, fever, colds and a cough
- Value: used as a diuretic.

Green brier - Smilax rotundifolia
- Habitat: shady forests
- Height: tender vines under ½ inch wide on shrubs and trees up to 30 ft
- Leaves: the leaves are heart-shaped
- Flower: the green flowers are difficult to see
- Time: all year
- Use: vines and tendrils are steamed like a vegetable Tubers are sliced, pounded and boiled to release starch used as a thickener
- Nutritional value: contains nitrogen

Ground Cherries – Physalis Philadelphica   (Husk Tomatoes) eat only when ripe
- Habitat: fields, sunny woods, bordering streams, waste ground and road sides
- Height: 1 to 3 ft high
- Fruit: yellowish sticky berry in a husk and ripens off the plant
- Flower: flowers are yellow with dark centres
- Time: blossoms in late spring and bears fruit in fall
- Use: Has a unique tomato, pineapple like taste and used for gravy, jelly or jam
- Nutritional value: A good source of Vitamin A, C and B3 (Niacin).

Henbit - Lamium amplexicaule
- Habitat: on lawns, roadsides, vacant lots and in fields
- Height: up to 6 inches

- Leaves: small leaves
- Flower: purple flowers
- Time: early spring, fall and winter
- Use: in salads or greens

Honey locust tree seed pods - Gleditsia triacanthos
- Habitat: trees found in moist soil, river valleys and other places
- Height: up to 60ft tall trees, often very old
- Seed pods: long brown curved pods with a sweet date-like pulp inside
- Time: Fall
- Use: Seed pods may be dried and ground into sweet flour
  The paste in the pods may be scraped off and used like dates
- Nutritional value: contains proteins and carbohydrates.

Indian cucumber - Medeola virginiana
- Habitat: grows in open woods and forests
- Height: 1 to 2 feet tall
- Leaves: 6 smooth leaves in a star like shape with a second level of 3 more on top
- Flower: yellow, small flower, hanging down
- Time: Blooms in late summer or early fall
- Use: tubers (roots) are edible raw and taste like cucumbers.

Jerusalem artichokes - Helianthus tuberosus
- Habitat: roadsides, vacant lots and fields
- Height: up to 10 feet tall
- Leaves: ovate leaves 5 to 10 inches long
- Flower: flower has 10 to 20 bright yellow petals
- Time: blossoms in late summer and early fall Pick tubers two weeks after flowers fade
- Use: tubers grated raw into salads or used as potatoes
- Nutritional value: are high in iron, and contain potassium, fibre, niacin, thiamine, phosphorus and copper.

Living in Difficult Times

Kudzu
- Habitat: It is a climbing, coiling, and trailing vine along roadsides
- Height: it covers vast low areas, shrubs and high trees
- Leaves: consist of 3 leaflets arranged alternately along the stem
- Flower: Pink coloured
- Time: has leaf foliage and flowers throughout spring and summer
- Use: flowers are used to make pink lemonade and the roots as a starch Leaves can be deep fried like potato chips
- Nutritional value: high-protein food similar to alfalfa.

Lambs quarters - Chenopodium album
- Habitat: lawns, roadsides, vacant lots and fields
- Height: 1 to 4ft
- Leaves: dark green diamond shaped
- Flower: the small green flowers come in dense spikes at the top
- Time: spring to fall
- Use: in salads, or steamed 5 to 10 minutes like spinach In summertime flower heads can be used in casseroles and breads
- Nutritional value: source of beta-carotene, calcium, potassium, and iron.

Lettuce saxiphrage - Saxifraga Montana
- Habitat: between rocks or in marshes, moist meadows and brooks
- Height: up to 24 inches tall
- Leaves: a green 1ft rosette of leaves close to ground – like a deer's tongue
- Flower: clusters of white blossoms at the top
- Time: spring through summer
- Use: leaves picked before flowering, used in salads, greens, soups or with eggs and bacon when dried, the leaves have a vanilla fragrance.

Magnolia - Magnolia virginiana
  - Habitat: these are deciduous, evergreen trees grown in garden settings
  - Height: up to 40 feet high
  - Leaves: large glossy leaves
  - Flower: drooping cup shaped flowers that are white or pink
  - Time: Springtime after the leaves emerge
  - Use: Fragrant smelling flowers with petals that may be used in salads
  - Nutritional value: the white blossoms are said to be antispasmodic and a tonic.

Meadowsweet - Filipendula ulmaria
  - Habitat: grows in damp meadows
  - Height: 3 to 7 ft tall
  - Leaves: leaflets are up to 3 inches long with three to five lobes
  - Flower: has creamy-white flower clusters close together, having a sweet smell
  - Time: June to September
  - Use: flowers can be added to stewed fruit and jams, giving them an almond flavour
  - Nutritional value: includes flavonoids such as flavonol glycosides, rutin, hyperin, spiraeoside as well as mucilage, carbohydrates, ascorbic acid, sugars and minerals.

Mullein - Verbascum Thapsus
  - Habitat: along roadsides and fields
  - Height: has a single stem up to 7 ft tall
  - Leaves: silvery leaves up to 19 inches long and 5 inches wide
  - Flower: a pinnacle of many 5-petalled bright yellow flowers at the top
  - Time: flowering June to August
  - Use: Leaves used as an antihistamine for colds, coughs and related problems

- Value: a tea made from the leaves coats and soothes mucus membranes in both the respiratory and digestive tracts. Its slimy consistency when in contact with water, coats and helps to treat existing ulcers in the stomach and intestines. It also relieves irritation caused by coughing spasms.

Mustard (field) - Cleome viscose
- Habitat: old pastures, gardens, lawns and the roadside
- Height: up to 2 ft
- Leaves: lobed
- Flower: four yellow petals in the form of a cross
- Time: springtime
- Use: young leaves in salads, leaves cooked as a potherb and seeds used as a spice
- Nutritional value: contains proteins, carbohydrates and fibre.

Plantain - Plantago major
- Habitat: roadsides, vacant lots and fields
- Height: oval leaf grows close to the ground
- Leaves: narrow or oval leaves
- Flower: pencil-shaped flower stalks
- Time: spring to fall – use the tender leaves before it flowers
- Use: with salads, greens or fried rice
- Cooking time: Boil and strain twice to improve the flavour
- Nutritional value: High in dietary fibre, potassium and Vitamins A, C and B6.

Poke - Phytolacca decandra
- Habitat: roadsides, vacant lots and fields
- Height: 4 to 8 ft tall
- Leaves: smooth-edged, green leaves 8 to 10 inches long
- Time: spring
- Use: eat only the young stems and leaves in the spring, less than 8 inches tall
- Cooking time: boil and rinse at least three times. May be scrambled with eggs.

Purslane - Portulaca oleracea
- Habitat: sprawling on lawns and in meadows
- leaves: paddle-shaped, succulent, stalk-less, up to 2 inches long, creeping up to 10 inches
- Flower: tiny flowers with five yellow petals
- Time: mid-summer to fall
- Use: leaves and stems, raw in salads. Steamed or added to soups or stews
- Nutritional value: is very low in calories and fats; but is rich in dietary fibre, vitamins, and minerals.

Queen Anne's lace - Daucus carota
- Habitat: lawns, roadsides, vacant lots and fields
- Height: 2 to 4ft tall
- Leaves: leaves have a smell similar to carrots and the leaf stalks are fuzzy
- Flower: umbrella like, with many tiny white flowers that looks like lace
- Time: early spring to fall
- Use: use the roots like a carrot in soups, stews, cakes and cookies
- Nutritional value: High in vitamin A, beta carotene and minerals

Warning - Hemlock is a poisonous look alike. Its green stem is usually spotted or streaked with red or purple on the lower half of the stem. When crushed, the leaves and root emit an unpleasant smell

Ramps (wild leek) - Allium tricoccum
- Habitat: in moist, open woodlands
- Height: 6 inches to 2ft tall
- Leaves: oval, smooth-edged, stalked leaves, 4 to12 inches long and 2 inches wide
- Flower: small, umbrella-like 6 petal white-cream colour flowers
- Time: spring through summer
- Use: the leaves or bulbs are used raw or cooked like garlic. (5 to 10 minutes)
- Nutritional value: contain Vitamins A, C, chromium and selenium.

Reed grass - Phragmites Communis
- Habitat: wetlands, meadows and marshes
- Height: 2 to 5ft tall
- Leaves: deep green shiny foliage
- Flower: feathery flowers in June
- Time: spring through winter
- Use: roots may be cut, boiled and leached for starch
- Nutritional value: It has protein and energy value.

Sassafras - Sassafras albidum
- Habitat: found on edges of forests or in thickets
- Height: smaller and larger trees
- Leaves: 3 oval, hand shaped leaves 3 to 5 inches long that smell like root beer
- Flowers: tiny, yellow, 5 petal flowers
- Time: leaves in spring through summer – leafless twigs in winter
- Use: leaves or twigs make a delicious tea.

Sheep sorrel - Rumex acetosella
- Habitat: is found in fields, grasslands, woodlands, flood-plains or marshes
- Height: about 16 to 18 inches tall
- Leaves: have green arrowhead shaped leaves
- Flower: yellow-green flowers
- Time: flowers March through September
- Use: a lemon flavour used in garnishes or salads and as a curdling agent for cheese
- Nutritional value: Is high in vitamins A, B, C, D, K and E. It also has calcium, iron, silicon, magnesium, suphur, zinc, manganese, iodine, beta carotene, copper and is rich in potassium oxalate. It also has great medicinal value.

Shepherds purse - Capsella bursa-pastoris
- Habitat: sprawling on lawns, in meadows, roadsides, vacant lots and fields
- Height: flower stalk grows up to 2½ ft tall with wedge shaped fruit pods

- Leaves: a rosette of bottom leaves up to 9 inches across like a dandelion
- Flower: tiny, white, 4-petaled flowers on a stalk
- Time: spring through fall
- Use: raw in salads, simmered in soups, stews and sauces Sauté, steam or cook for about 10 minutes
- Nutritional value: contains compounds like alkaloids, histamine, flavonoids, thiamine, organic acids, phenols, volatile oils and salts and vitamins. Shepherd's purse has analeptic properties and can regulate blood pressure.

Sochan - Rudbeckia laciniata
- Habitat: along trails, roadways, in wet meadows and alongside streams
- Height: up to 5 ft
- Leaves: alternating hairy leaves
- Flower: yellow clusters of flowers in late summer
- Time: spring to summer
- Use: tender spring leaves for greens and the young stems like celery
- Nutritional value: eaten as a healthy vegetable.

Solomon seal - Polygonatum multiflorum
- Habitat: in moist and rocky woods and thickets
- Height: up to 2ft
- Leaves: light green broad ovate leaves
- Flower colour: light yellow green clusters of drooping flowers
- Time: flowers in spring
- Use: roots are boiled and eaten like asparagus after 3 changes of water
- Nutritional value: it has saponins, flavonoids and vitamin A.

Sorrel - Oxalis acetosella
- Habitat: on lawns, in meadows, roadsides, vacant lots and fields
- Height: up to 8 inches tall
- Leaves: shaped like hearts

- Flower: small five-petal yellow flowers
- Time: early spring to late fall
- Use: in salads, in soups, stews or a tea
- Nutritional value: is rich in Vitamin C, niacin, riboflavin and thiamin.

Spice bush - Lindera benzoin
- Habitat: damp shaded woods, low mountain slopes, thickets and streams
- Height: up to 20 ft tall releasing a lemon-spicy fragrance
- Leaves: bright green, alternate, toothless, elliptical leaves 2 to 6 inches long
- Fruit: ripe berries, finely chopped, are used as a seasoning that tastes like allspice
- Time: spring to fall
- Use: berries sliced with apples, walnuts, orange rind, simmered for 15 minutes and used in pies. Leaves or twigs used to make a tea
- Nutritional value: Young branches may be steeped to make a tonic.

Stevia - Stevia rebaudiana
- Habitat: found in moist sandy soils, often near the edge of marshes or streams
- Height: a perennial shrub that grows up to 40 inches tall
- Leaves: tongue shaped and slightly serrated up to 1 inch long
- Flower: small white flowers
- Time: from mid-summer to late fall
- Use: used as a sweetener or sugar substitute
- Nutritional value: has many health benefiting plant-derived phyto-chemical compounds that help control blood sugar, cholesterol and blood pressure.

Stinging nettle - Urtica dioica
(Do not handle with bare hands as they have invisible stinging hairs)
- Habitat: disturbed soil, moist woodlands, thickets, along rivers or on partially shaded trails
- Height: 2 to 4 ft tall

- Leaves: leaves are opposite each other, pointed, dark green, about 2 inches long with a heart-shaped base
- Time: spring through fall
- Use: cook for 30 minutes for a soup or as greens (Cooking for 6 minutes in boiling water will neutralize any toxicity in the plant)
- Nutritional value: contains lots of proteins, large amounts of chlorophyll, vitamin A, several B's, C, D and an abundance of minerals including calcium, iron, manganese, phosphorus, potassium, silicon and sulphur.

Sumac - Rhus trilobata
- Habitat: in meadows, roadsides, vacant lots and fields
- Height: a shrub or small tree
- Leaves: large leaves, divided into 11 to 23 leaflets
- Fruit: hangs in bunches and are red, short and hairy
- Time: fruits summer to fall
- Use: ripe berries soaked in boiling water for about 2 minutes, filtered and sweetened as lemonade.

Sweet gum tree - Liquidambar styraciflua
- Habitat: commonly found in swamps and near ponds and streams
- Height: up to 100ft tall
- Leaves: five-pointed star-shaped, dark green glossy leaves up to 6 inches long
- Flower: greenish flowers
- Time: flowers March through May
- Use: Pioneers peeled the bark, scraping the resin solids to use as chewing gum.

Sweet birch tree - Betula lenta
- Habitat: fields and forests
- Height: tree growing up to 60ft
- Leaves: dark shiny green, 2 to 4 inches long and have a wintergreen smell
- Flowers: green male catkins that are near the end of the twig
- Time: spring through fall

- Use: Boil and simmer the bark, leaves and twigs as a sweet, aromatic tea
- Nutritional value: serves as a sugar substitute.

Watercress - Nasturtium officinale
- Habitat: in country streams and fresh running water from 2 to 6 inches deep
- Height: creeping rootstock, 1 to 2 feet in length with its leaves above the water
- Leaves: smooth, fleshy, dark green, with 1 to 4 pairs of small, round leaves
- Time: best gathered in spring through summer before it flowers
- Use: in salads, soups and casseroles
- Nutritional value: is low in Saturated Fat and Cholesterol. It has Proteins, Folate, Pantothenic Acid and Copper. Is a great source of Vitamin A, B6, C, E (Alpha Tocopherol), Vitamin K, Thiamin, Riboflavin, Calcium, Magnesium, Phosphorus, Potassium and Manganese.

Wild garlic - Allium vineale
- Habitat: grows in deciduous woodlands, moist or sandy soils
- Height: up to 24 inches tall
- Leaves: round, hollow, arising from a bulb, up to 24 inches long and 3 inches wide
- Flowers: small greenish white flowers at the top of the flowering stem
- Time: flowers in spring
- Use: small egg-shaped bulbs used as garlic
- Nutritional value: when pure it yields strong smelling oil, essence of garlic, composed of diallyl sulphide $(C_3H_5)_2S$.

Wild lettuce – Lactuca serriola
- Habitat: a common widespread weed
- Height: up to 5 ft tall
- Leaves: bluish green leaves are deeply lobed with pokey prickles along the edges
- Flowers: are yellow in colour

- Time: Flower in summer
- Use: leaves used in salads and cooked as greens
  Plant may also be used as a mild opiate for pain
- Nutritional value: Source of vitamin A, potassium and nutrients.

Wild onions - A.validum
- Habitat: on lawns, roadsides, vacant lots and fields
- Height: up to 2 ft tall
- Leaves: Leaves are narrow and long, arising from a small underground bulb
- Flower: white or pink appearing in late summer
- Time: Spring and Fall
- Use: the same way as regular onions
- Nutritional value: Contains proteins, carbohydrates, calcium, magnesium, zink, manganese, phosphorous. Also has choline, chromium, niacin, riboflavin, folate, carotene and vitamins A, B6 and C.

Wild strawberry -
- Habitat: grows in forests, fields, lawns, forest edges, roadsides and along streams
- Height: up to 1ft tall
- Leaves: pale green trifoliate leaves that emerge directly from the centre
- Flowers: have 5 white petals
- Fruit: similar but smaller than regular strawberries
- Time: Spring and Fall
- Use: may be used in cereal, pancakes, fruit salad, sauces or deserts
- Nutritional value: is low in sodium, saturated Fat and cholesterol. It is a very good
source of Vitamin C.

Yarrow - Achillea Millefolium
- Habitat: in meadows, roadsides, vacant lots and fields
- Height: 2 to 5ft
- Leaves: green feathery, fern-like
- Flower: white flattened flower clusters up to 6 inches wide

- Time: blooming occurs June through September
- Use: flowers boiled and simmered to make a tea
- Nutritional value: contains fibre and proteins

Yellow wood sorrel - Oxalis stricta
- Habitat: on lawns, in meadows, roadsides, vacant lots and fields
- Height: up to 12 inches tall
- Leaves: light green alternate trifoliate leaves about ¾ inch across when fully open
- Flower: yellow flowers about ½ inch in diameter
- Time: Spring through Fall
- Use: added to salads, soups, with fish or brewed to make a kind of lemonade
- Nutritional value: contains vitamin C.

Yucca - Yucca Filamentosa
- Habitat: dry areas
- Height: up to 6 feet tall
- Leaves: long dagger-like leaves
- Flower: white flowers that are tulip-like, waxy, and drooping
- Time: late spring
- Use: flower petals raw in salads, fried or batter dipped
- Nutritional value: contains vitamin C, calcium and carbohydrates.

Wild Mushrooms

Disclaimer
Be sure to visit a mushroom club in your area, where you can learn everything you need to know about fungi.
You should not eat any mushroom unless you can identify it and are absolutely certain that it is not poisonous.
Reading and using information in this book will constitute your acceptance of this disclaimer.

Puff ball (giant) - Calvatia gigantea
- Habitat: grows on the ground or on dead wood
- Size: small to a football size
- Time: spring through fall
- Use: sautéed, simmered in soups, cooked up to 12 minutes with grains or baked in a casserole
- Description: puffballs are round, white, soft inside and like cream cheese or tofu.

Morel - Morchella
- Habitat: in woods and on trails in small patches
- Size: 2 to 10 inches tall
- Time: in spring and comes up after forest fires
- Use: sauté and use in soups, casseroles or stews
- Description: looks honeycombed and the cap is the length of the stalk
- Nutritional value: - contains proteins and carbohydrates.
Warning: don't eat morels raw and cook them for at least 15 minutes.

Wine cap - Auricularia polytricha
- Habitat: grows on the ground under oak and conifer trees
- Size: cap is 2 to 6 inches wide
- Time: summer through fall
- Use: grill, bake or add to soups. Cooks in 15 to 20 minutes
- Description: wine colour cap and bell-shaped
- Nutritional value: - contains proteins and carbohydrates.

Shitake - Lentinula edodes
- Size: cap is up to 4 inches wide
- Use: grill, bake or add to soups and salads
- Description: cultivated or available in stores
- Nutritional value: - Contains protein, Vitamins A, B2, B2, B6, B12, C, D2, E, K, niacin, carbohydrates, phosphorous, calcium, potassium and iron.

Dryad saddle - Polyporus squamosus
- Habitat: grows on living and dead hardwoods
- Size: 3 to 10 inches across and smells like watermelon
- Time: spring through fall (best to forage in May)
- Use: use when young in jambalaya, batter fried or in pasta primavera
- Description: kidney-shaped, overlapping brown caps that have darker scales on top.

Oyster - Pleurotus ostreatus
- Habitat: oyster-shaped caps that are layered, growing on dead deciduous wood
- Size: caps 2 to 6 inches wide
- Time: all year, especially spring and fall
- Use: cook the tender parts up to 18 minutes and use in seafood or salads
- Description: grows in shelf-like clusters and looks, smells, and tastes like oysters
- Nutritional value: Contains protein, Vitamins B2, B2, B3, carbohydrates, phosphorous, Calcium and iron.

Chanterelle - Cantharellus cibarius
- Habitat: grows on the ground under oak and conifer trees
- Size: up to 5 inches wide and has a fruity fragrance
- Colour: bright orange or yellow
- Time: summer through fall
- Use: in salads, omelette's and stews
- Description: vase-shaped, funnel-like mushrooms
- Nutritional value: contains carbohydrates.

Hen of the woods - Grifola frondosa
- Habitat: grows at the base of oak trees or on stumps

- Size: can grow up to 60 lbs
- Time: fall
- Use: cook and serve as a vegetable with cream sauce
- Description: it overlaps in a form of a bouquet.

Scaber stalk (red capped) - Leccinum aurantiacum
- Habitat: grows under birch trees
- Size: 1 to 4 inches
- Time: summer through fall
- Use: stuffed, broiled with seasonings or used in gravy
- Description: sometimes sunken in the centre with white flesh When bruised becomes slightly brown
- Nutritional value: contain proteins, vitamins B1, B2, C, D, magnesium, iron and Calcium.

Meadow - Agaricus campestris
- Habitat: grows on lawns, pastures and in open areas
- Size: 2 to 4 inches wide
- Time: in late summer
- Use: add to soups stews and salads
- Description: Like the white button mushroom, a pale white or light brown colour
- Nutritional value: a good source of vitamins B, Potassium, Phosphorus and Selenium

Warning - Do not confuse with the poisonous Agaricus xanthodermis, which is similar in appearance. This poisonous mushroom has a stem that bruises yellow at the base when cut or bruised.

Horse - Agaricus arvensis
- Habitat: grows on lawns, pastures and in open areas
- Size: Thick, white firm flesh cap, 3 to 10 inches wide with fine scales
- Time: in the late summer
- Use: add to soups, stews and salads
- Description: White and turning a slight tan as they mature, with a brown scale patch on the top centre. Only use the younger horse mushrooms that have a cogwheel pattern on the broken veil

- Nutritional value: a good source of vitamins B, D, Potassium, Phosphorus and Selenium.

Warning - Do not confuse with the poisonous Agaricus xanthodermis, which is similar in appearance. This poisonous mushroom has a stem that bruises yellow at the base when cut or bruised.

Prince - Agaricus augustus
- Habitat: is found in deciduous, coniferous woods and in gardens or by roadsides
- Size: white to tan caps up to 8 inches wide, with brownish flat scales
- Time: in the Fall
- Use: grill, bake or add to soups and salads
- Description: The flesh is thick, firm and white with a strong almond smell like anise
- Nutritional value: low in calories, cholesterol-free, fat-free, low in sodium content with vitamins B, D, potassium and selenium.

Bolette -
- Habitat: grows on the ground under oak, conifer trees and pine needles
- Size: 1 inch and larger caps
- Time: most common in summer
- Use: young mushrooms may be sautéed and used in sauces, meat and fish dishes
- Descriptions: A variation of colours, umbrella shaped with a cap and a stalk
- Nutritional value: rich in proteins, vitamins and minerals.

Warning: Those with red spores must be avoided.

Suggested book to research:
Edible wild mushrooms of North America -
(A field to kitchen guide: by David W Fischer & Alan Bessette)

Websites worth visiting:
http://foragingguide.com/
http://www.wildernesscollege.com/poisonous-mushrooms.html

Nuts

Walnut - Juglans nigra
- Habitat: in meadows, roadsides and fields
- Tree: dark brown with a deeply furrowed bark
- Leaves: lance-shaped 3 inch leaflets
- Flowers: small green flowers
- Time: walnuts fall to the ground September to October
- Use: peeled, boiled, cleaned and also dried and ground for flour
- Nut description: Shells are tough with grooves and contain a small kernel inside
- Nutritional value: contains riboflavin, niacin, thiamin, pantothenic acid, vitamin B6, and folates. Also is a rich source of manganese, copper, potassium, calcium, iron, magnesium, zinc, and selenium. It has many phyto-chemical substances that may contribute to their overall anti-oxidant activity, including melatonin, ellagic acid, vitamin E, carotenoids, and poly-phenolic compounds.

Pecan - Carya illinoinensis
- Habitat: in meadows, roadsides and fields
- Tree height: up to 120 ft
- Time: in fall
- Use: used in pecan pies, dessert, praline candy or making pecan butter
- Nut description: smooth, tan, tough shell, 1 inch in length and a tasty kernel inside
- Nutritional value: It contains oleic acid and antioxidants including polyphenolic antioxidant ellagic acid, vitamin E, beta-carotenes, lutein and zeaxanthin. It is packed with the B-complex groups of vitamins - riboflavin,

niacin, thiamin, pantothenic acid, vitamin B-6, and folates. It has minerals like manganese, potassium, calcium, iron, magnesium, zinc, and selenium.

Hickory - Carya glabra
- Habitat: in meadows, roadsides and fields
- Tree height: up to 130ft
- Time: it falls to the ground in December
- Use: in baking products and as a pecan substitute
- Nut description: thick and tough shell and the kernel is in 2 parts
- Nutritional value: contains phosphorus, calcium and fibre.

Acorn - Quercus Alba
- Habitat: in meadows, roadsides and fields
- Tree height: up to 130ft
- Time: in fall and may be dried and stored for long periods
- Use: ground for flour and to make noodles
- Nut description: a tough leathery shell in a cup shaped cupule with a single kernel
- Nutritional value: contains nitrogen, calcium, protein and fibre.

Beech – (American beech) - Fagus grandifolia
- Habitat: in meadows, roadsides and fields
- Tree height: up to 80ft
- Time: picked from the tree before they fall – September through November
- Use: a tasty snack
- Nut description: a small sharp 3 angled nut inside a soft-spine husk
- Nutritional value: Nuts are a valuable source of nutrition.

Chestnut – Castanea
- Habitat: In fields and on mountains
- Tree height: up to 100ft tall

- Leaves: are ovate and lanced up to 10 inches long and 3 inches wide
- Time: enjoyed from fall through winter
- Use: nuts may be roasted and eaten or used as a cereal or flour
- Nut description: the burrs are paired on the branches and contain up to seven nuts
- Nutritional value: contains vitamins A. C, carbohydrates, proteins, fibre, foltes, niacin, panthothenic acid, pyridoxine, riboflavin, thiamin, sodium, potassium, calcium, copper, iron, mangenes, magnesium, phosphorous and zink.

Fruit

Crab-apples - Malus angustifolia
- Habitat: in meadows, roadsides, fields and on mountains
- Height: up to 30ft tall
- Leaves: are small and pale green
- Flower: range from white to pink
- Fruit: are small, tart and yellow to red when ripe, growing in dense clusters
- Time: late summer
- Use: cooked with sugar, makes a red jelly that may be used with toast, scones and other baked foods
- Nutritional value: contains Vitamin A, C and calcium.

Pawpaw - Asimina
- Habitat: at deep fertile bottom lands or hilly uplands
- Tree height: clustered trees up to 30ft high
- Leaves: large, alternate, ovate leaves
- Time: Fall
- Use: eaten as fruit, in desserts and for juices
- Fruit description: yellow-brown, 6 inches long and tastes like mango and banana
- Nutritional value: they are high in vitamin C, magnesium, iron, copper and manganese. They also have potassium, essential amino acids, riboflavin, niacin, calcium, phosphorus, zinc and antioxidant properties.

Persimmon - Diospyros virginiana
- Habitat: in meadows and fields
- Tree height: a small tree
- Leaves: broad stiff leaves
- Time: late fall
- Use: eaten when ripe and soft (slightly tangy) Used for desserts, for baking, jams or dried as a snack
- Fruit description: yellow to red-orange colour about 3 inches and acorn in shape
- Nutritional value: has vitamin A and C.

Passion vine - Passiflora Incarnata
- Habitat: in meadows, roadsides, vacant lots and fields
- Vine height: a shrub-like vine with a beautiful 10 leaf flower
- Leaves: 4 inch lance like leaves
- Time: summer
- Use: fruit in salads and as a snack
- Fruit description: shiny yellow-orange round fruit – partially hollow
- Nutritional value: has vitamin A and niacin.

Wild cherry - Prunus avium
- Habitat: in meadows, vacant lots and fields
- Tree height: up to 40 ft tall
- Leaves: serrated margin leaves
- Use: for jelly or jam. The gum of the bark is a chewing gum substitute
- Fruit description: a sweetish red astringent fruit eaten when very ripe
- Nutritional value: has vitamins C, A and antioxidants.

Muscadine - Vitis vinifera
- Habitat: in meadows, roadsides, vacant lots and fields
- Vine height: like grape vines
- Leaves: slightly lobed 5 inch leaves
- Time: mid summer

- Use: To eat as grapes or to make jelly and wine
- Fruit description: dark green or purple grapes with a thick skin
- Nutritional value: contains vitamin C, fibre, proteins, potassium, calcium, magnesium, antioxidants, phyto-chemicals and beneficial oils.

Bunch berry - Cornus canadensis
- Habitat: in meadows, roadsides, vacant lots and fields
- Height: up to 39 inches high
- Leaves: 6 leaf, star shaped floret with flowers or berries in the centre
- Flowers: have 4 white petals
- Time: late summer
- Use: to make jams, preserves, sauces, syrups and candy
- Fruit description: bright red drupes with mild flavour like apples
- Has nutritional value.

Blackberry (American) - Rubus villosus
- Habitat: in thickets, along roadsides, trail edges and fields
- Vine height: up to 9 ft tall
- Leaves: 3 to 7 sharply-toothed leaflets
- Flowers: have 5 white petals
- Time: mid-summer to early fall
- Use: in pies, fruit salads or juice
- Fruit description: black berries when ripe
- Nutritional value: contains dietary fibre, vitamins B, C, K, folic acid, antioxidants and polyphenolic compounds such as ellagic acid, tannins, ellagitannins, quercetin, gallic acid, anthocyanins and cyanidins.

Blueberry
- Habitat: in meadows, vacant lots and fields
- Height: up to 13 ft tall
- Leaves: evergreen, ovate, lance-like, 3 inches long and 2 inches wide

- Flower: bell-shaped, white, pale-pink or red
- Fruit: purple berries up to ½ inch in diameter
- Time: May through August
- Use: eaten as a fruit or used for juice, pancakes or pies
- Nutritional value: very low in Saturated Fat, Cholesterol and Sodium. It is good source of Dietary Fibre, and a very good source of Vitamin C, Vitamin K and Manganese.

Mulberry - Morus nigra
- Habitat: in meadows, vacant lots and fields
- Tree height: up to 40ft tall
- Leaves: alternate lobed leaves
- Time: summer
- Use: used in pies, fruit salads, jams and for juice
- Fruit description: purple-black when ripe
- Nutritional value: contains vitamins A, C, E and many other health promoting flavonoid poly phenolic antioxidants such aslutein, zeaxanthin, b-carotene and a-carotene.

Fox grape - Vitix labrusca
- Habitat: in meadows, vacant lots and fields
- Vine height: up to 5ft
- Leaves: typical serrated grape vine leaves
- Time: late summer through fall
- Use: for dried fruit, cookies and candy
- Fruit description: similar to blueberries
- Nutritional value typical to grapes.

Herbs

Herbs have distinctive flavours.

When used in everyday meals they invigorate cooking.

They enhance the tastes and cuisine of salads and special dishes being prepared.

Herbs can be planted in pots and conveniently kept indoors during the cold months.

Here are some of the herbs worth growing and using for culinary purposes:

Sage - Salvia officinalis

Sage is an evergreen shrub and can reach a height of 2 feet. It varies in colour from gray to green, with one variety producing deep purple leaves.

It has camphor scented, purple-blue flowers, which appear in mid-summer.

It enhances Tomato, Eggplant, and Bean dishes.

It is a traditional herb also used in poultry stuffing.

It may be chopped and sautéed with Onions, Garlic and with a squeeze of Lemon juice added to pasta.

Cilantro – Coriandrum sativum

Cilantro is a pungent annual herb that closely resembles parsley and grows up to 6 inches high. It is commonly used for sauces. The leaves of cilantro are light green, feathery, flat and have a distinctive flavour. The dried seeds, called coriander seed, are used as a spice and have an entirely different taste.

Sweet Basil – Ocimum basilicum

It is an annual plant with highly aromatic leaves that have a pleasant spicy door odour

It may be generously used in sauces.

Oregano – Origanum vulgare

It grows to a height of about 8 inches with woody stems and dark green leaves with small, white flowers. It may be added to salads, casseroles, soups, sauces, pates and poultry dishes.

Dried oregano is especially good with tomatoes, beans, egg-plant, zucchini and rice dishes such as pilaf and risotto. One should always add oregano in the last few minutes of cooking otherwise its flavour can become bitter.

Thyme – Thymus vulgaris
It grows six to twelve inches in height. The leaves are dark gray-green in colour, and pale pink flowers bloom at the tips of the stems in summer.
Thyme has a strong piquant, lemony flavour which is best just before flowering.
This herb enhances the flavour of meat, fish and poultry dishes. It may be used for chicken and fish marinades and in herb butters and cottage cheese.
The fresh sprigs of thyme may also be combined with red-wine vinegar and olive oil for flavouring.

Dill – Anethum graveolens
Dill grows up to 3 feet tall
A sprig of dill always perks up any main dish and is wonderful in a dip, herb butter, soups, fish dishes, and salads.
The seeds are used in pickling.

Parsley – Petroselinum crispum
Parsley is a hardy annual plant. It has the appearance of a small bush and has deep green crinkled leaves. It grows up to 12 inches high.
It is commonly used in a variety of recipes of hot casseroles and cold salads. It can be used either freshly cut or dried and ground.

Rosemary - Rosmarinus officinalis
Rosemary grows to a height of up to 5 feet. It has pine nee-dle-like leaves with blue flowers through summer. It is won-derful with lamb and sprigs of the herb are tucked into slits made in the lamb for roasting. Chopped leaves may also be used sparingly in soups, food dishes and stews.

Foraging food on beaches

Beach walking is a refreshing experience where one may forage nourishing food.

When foraging, be sure to forage on unpolluted beaches that have few visitors.

The best time to pick up different types of sea plants is after the tide has come in.

Food also may be found clinging to rocks, in the water, lying on the beach or floating in tidal pools.

Different foods are found at different times of the year.

You may need a knife, fork, bucket to forage and always follow the rules of foraging.

A good regional guide will help you identify edible plants, shellfish and the important information you need to be successful.

Remember -

Never eat anything you cannot identify as safe to eat!

Do not disturb surrounding plants or animal life and only take what you will use!

Pictures of most of these may be found when doing an online web search.

South Atlantic beaches

Oysters - Crassostrea virginicus

They are exposed at low tide on the grass of rock banks, or in tidal marsh areas.

Oysters may be eaten raw by inserting a blunt knife into the clamped edge, moving it side-to-side to force it open. Use gloves to prevent cuts from the sharp shell.

Once open, simply trim out the meat and enjoy.

They may be cooked with other sea-food or used in oyster soup.

Nutrition value: Contains fat, carbohydrates, proteins, calcium, iron and zink.

Glasswort (American) - Salicornia virginica
It is a low succulent plant about eight inches high with branching, jointed tendrils that have a salty sap. It is also called "beach asparagus."
It may be used in a salad after boiling the tendrils for just a few minutes until tender.
Glasswort may be picked in July before it gets tough.
Nutrition value: contain high levels of unsaturated oil, linoleic acid and protein.

Sea rocket - Cakile maritima
It is used to flavour sea-foods, salads and tastes like horseradish. It is a low, fleshy plant with succulent branching stems. It has pointed seed pods that form after the late-summer flowers that are lavender in colour. They may be found along the high-tide marks on sand beaches, after being washed up and germinated on shore. The fleshy root may be dried and ground and used as an additive to bread flour.
The chopped leaves and stems may be cooked with other vegetables and seafood, or added raw to a salad.
Nutrition value: contains iodine, calcium, magnesium, iron, vitamins, flavonoids and antioxidants.

Sea lettuce – ulva genus
Sea lettuce grows in sheets of green plant material about 3 feet in length.
It has slightly wavy edges and is usually found in smaller pieces, washed up on the beach. It can be sliced raw into salads, cooked into soups or sautéed with onions and other vegetables.
Nutrition value: contains magnesium, potassium, calcium, phosphorus, iron, manganese, vitamin A and B-3.

West Coast beaches

Kelp - Macrocystis pyrifera
It has a long and wavy central frond about six inches wide, growing up to 10 feet high. It may be found in the surging ocean during low tide, in thick beds anchored to the rocks.

It is green or brown and often found floating freely in the water. It is a healthy and tasty additive to chowders, soups and stews.
Nutrition value: contains iodine, potassium, proteins and carbohydrates.

Butter clams - Saxidomus gigantea
They are found in shallow water sand. At low tide, they are often found in the sand where shells are lying on the beach. A tiny jet of water shooting from the sand will betray their presence. Dig a few inches deep and find them.
Steam the clams for 3-5 minutes.
If some don't open while being steamed, discard them.
Nutrition value: contains selenium, zinc, iron, magnesium and niacin.

Hottentot figs - Carpobrotus edulis
It is a succulent plant with long, trailing stems. It has yellow daisy-like flowers that turn pink and grow in mats. It may be found on sand dunes. By July the flowers start forming a fleshy, fig-like brown fruit that makes a wonderful jam.
Add two cups of sugar to a cup of hottentot figs.
Boil and stir until it becomes like syrup.
It may be used over cereal or pancakes.
Has nutritional value.

Dulse - Palmaria palmate
It is edible seaweed to be eaten when cooked.
It is algae that is a translucent purple-red, with foot-long leafy, flat lobes.
It is found clustered on rocky shores exposed during the low tide and in sheltered lagoons, away from the surging sea. It is a delicate plant, and may be pulled from the rocks by hand. It may be cooked with soups and chowders.
It is rubbery if eaten raw, but has a pleasing texture after drying in the sun and is a natural source of iodine.
Nutrition value: contains iodine, calcium, zinc, vitamin A, B6, B12, C, iron, chromium, riboflavin and niacin.

Beach strawberries – fragaria chiloensis
It grows up to eight inches high, with trifoliate toothed leaves and red berries that ripen through midsummer. They are found on sand dunes and have five-petal white blossoms, which bloom into a ripening fruit. The berries may be eaten raw, cooked to a jam or mixed with bread and pancake batter. The berries and the leaves may be used to make a tasty tea.
Nutrition value: high in vitamin C.

Sea lettuce – ulva genus
Sea lettuce grows in green sheets about 3 feet long, with wavy edges.
It is usually found in smaller pieces, washed up on the beach.
It can be sliced raw into salads, cooked in soups or sautéed with onions and vegetables.
Nutrition value: contains magnesium, potassium, calcium, phosphorus, iron, manganese, vitamin A and B-3.

North Atlantic beaches

Blue Mussels - Mytilus edulis
Cling to rocks or are found on the surface of the sand, just below the half-tide line.
Nutrition value: Proteins, carbohydrates, fat, fibre, selenium and zink.

Surf clams - Spisula solidissima -
Are found three to six inches deep in the mud or sea sand
A tiny jet of water shooting from the sand will betray their presence.
Dig a few inches deep and find them.
Steam the clams for 3-5 minutes.
If some don't open while being steamed, discard them.
Nutrition value: contains selenium, zinc, iron, magnesium and niacin.

Irish moss - Sagina subulata
It is algae up to six inches high with flat, forked fronds and has a leathery texture when freshly picked. It may be foraged by wading along the low-tide mark and gently pulling the plant free. It is found in mats in shallow tide-pools with colours ranging from green to purple brown.
When boiled up to 50 minutes, it becomes a gelatinous pudding with a sea flavour.
It may be topped with ice cream or cream and sugar.
Nutrition value: contains calcium, iodine, and potassium and vitamins A, D, E and K.

Beach peas - lathyrus japonicus
It is a trailing green plant with purple flowers with 2 inch pods
It may be found behind ridges of beach grass, or on the beach after storms.
It is best picked in August when the pods ripen and may be eaten as garden peas.
Has nutritional value

Scotch lovage - Ligusticum scoticum
(Known as sea lovage and wild beach celery and has pinkish-white blossoms in July)
It is like parsley and grows up to two feet high with glossy, dark-green leaves.
It has a pungent taste like parsley or celery leaves.
It grows among beach grasses or along the edge of salt marshes.
It is found from New England to Nova Scotia, and also in Alaska.
It is excellent with seafood.
Nutrition value: has vitamin A

Orach (Mountain Spinach) - Atriplex hortensis
It is vine like with two-inch arrowhead-shaped leaves, and grows in salt-rich sand.
It may be prepared like spinach, salad greens or with scrambled eggs.

Nutrition value: proteins, carbohydrates, fibre, ash, and b-carotene equivalent.

Ingredients for a Seaweed Salad
2 tbsp of rice vinegar
1 tbsp of soy sauce
1 tbsp of brown sugar
2 tbsp of sesame oil
Pour it over 4 cups of soaked, drained and shredded seaweed
Mix and garnish with 1 tbsp of toasted seed and serve

Most of these nourishing foods foraged on Beaches may be found near you.

Notes:

Chapter Six:
Menu ideas

Disclaimer
Experiencing enjoyment and success when using recipes in this book will depend on the following:

1. Using quality ingredients
2. Using the right utensils
3. Applying accurate temperatures
4. Following instructions correctly
5. Adjusting to the tastes, likes, dislikes or allergy requirements of its users

Vegetarians
Vegetarian ingredients may be substituted for other ingredients where necessary

Allergies
Those experiencing gluten allergies may substitute gluten free ingredients.
Those experiencing any other kind of allergy may substitute other ingredients.
Recipes may need to be modified accordingly.
Reading and using information in this book will constitute your acceptance of this disclaimer.

Use this chapter when planning your menu

Living in Difficult Times

Breakfast:

Any of the following -
Rolled, flattened cornmeal and then baked on a pan into flakes like cereal
Corn meal cooked as grits and served with milk, butter and sugar
Corn meal biscuits with sausage, egg, bacon, jam, honey or berries
Pancakes covered with honey or berries
Baked bread slices, toasted, buttered and covered with jam, honey or berries
Eggs made in different ways
Bacon made from hog, wild boar, chicken or turkey skin
Burrito's filled with egg, omelette, potato pieces, meat pieces and taco sauce
Italian sausage patties
Italian sausage links
Croissant soufflé
Breakfast pizza

Tea choices – (ingredients steeped in boiled water)
Elderberry leaves
Sassafras leaves
Sweet birch twigs
Yarrow leaves
Plantain leaves
Pine needles

Coffey choices – (steeped in boiled water)
Roasted and ground Chicory roots
Roasted and ground Dandelion roots
A combination of ground chicory, dandelion and beet roots

Lemonade choices – (crushed, steeped in water and sweetener added)
Dandelions
Sumac berries
Kudzu flowers
Elderberries
Sorrel leaves

Lunch or dinner choices:

Soup choices
Raw blended vegetable soup
Dandelion soup
Mushroom / Burdock soup
Cream of mushroom soup
Cream of onion soup
Cream of cattail soup
Cream of potato soup
Watercress bisque
Watercress soup
Chanterelle mushroom & leek soup
Amaranth soup
Stinging nettle soup
Wild onion bisque
Sheep sorrel soup
Curly Dock soup
Hickory nut soup
Bean soup
Vegetable soup
Chicken noodle soup
Cabbage soup
Meat broth or bisque

Salads and salad dressing choices
Mixed salads of any choice–
Lambs quarter leaves
Dandelion leaves
Chickweed leaves
Clover leaves
Watercress leaves
Purslane leaves
Blue violet leaves
Wild lettuce leaves
Sheep sorrel leaves
Wood sorrel leaves
Henbit leaves
Plantain leaves
Shepherds purse leaves
Curly dock leaves
Sassafras leaves
Yucca flowers
(Seeds / nuts / flower petals / vegetable substitutes / Dressing - may be added)

Greens choices
(Mixed greens or these individual greens, may be cooked, sautéed or curried)
Amaranth leaves
Chickweed leaves
Dandelion leaves
Poke leaves (Washed and rinsed three times)
Sheep sorrel leaves
Sochan leaves
Curly dock leaves
Lambs quarter leaves
Stinging nettle leaves (Do not touch with bare hands)
Ramps
Peeled Cactus leaves (Do not touch with bare hands)

Meal choices:

Meats –
Chicken / beef /mutton / lamb /goat
Wild turkey
Fish
Bird
Deer
Wild Boar
Squirrel
Turtle
Frog legs

Vegetable substitutes -
Wild Asparagus
Cattail heart
Green Brier Tendrils
Wild garlic & onions
Cattail stalks
Bamboo shoots
(Like beets or turnips)
Evening Primrose roots
(Like celery)
Sochan stems
(Like carrots or turnips)
Queen Anne lace roots
(Tubers that are like potatoes)
Jerusalem Artichoke
Orange/Yellow Daylily
Arrow head
(Like green beans)
Young Reed grass stems, Daylily unopened buds, Green
Brier Tendrils
(Like broccoli)
Milkweed flower buds or Wild mustard flower buds
(Like cucumbers or zucchini in thin slices)
Bamboo centres
Indian cucumber root
Cattail shoots harvested early
or
Wild mushrooms

Other meal choices
Sautéed peeled Cactus leaf, Peppers and Corn
Potatoes or their substitutes - raw
Curried Potatoes
Other potato preparations
Dandelion buds
Dandelion fritters
Wild onions
Chanterelle mushroom lasagne
Wild Mushroom Pasta Primavera
Savoury Wild Mushroom Bread Serving
Morel Quiche
Grilled Portobello Mushroom Steaks
Mushroom burgers
Chilli stuffed mushrooms
Trout
Potato Nests with sautéed Shitake or other Mushrooms

Meat -
Grilled / Stewed / Curried
Kebabs – with fruit or vegetables
Meatloaf
Hamburger sausage
Hamburger sausage – vegetarian
Italian Sausage
Chicken
Turkey
Chicken / Turkey pie
Bird - Pheasant / Grouse / Quail / Duck / Partridge/ Geese
Marinated duck
Fruit, curry and crispy duck
Pigeon
Rabbit stew
Rabbit pie
Rabbit roasting
Wild boar roasts
Wild boar stew
Wild boar sausage
Bacon
Wild boar quarters

Deer - Venison Stroganoff
Deer stew
Deer kebabs
Deer roast
Chickweed stew
Flower petal lamb delicacy
Turtle
Frog legs
Squirrel stew

Seafood
Cajun seafood gumbo
Watercress fish cakes
Crab cakes
Trout, Bass, Walleyes, Crappie, Catfish or other fish
Fish stuffing

Other
Stinging nettle fritters
Roll-ups
Bean pottage
Quiche
Soufflé croissants
Creamed watercress
Mushroom / onion / green beans casserole
Pizza
Pizza Toppings
Cornmeal biscuits
Pies
Soft and hard tacos
Fried squirrel cakes
Chicken Liver Pate
Mock Tuna (Pate)
Dumplings
Turnovers
Sushi
Oriental stir fry
Bread
Nuts
Indian Acorn Griddlecakes

Living in Difficult Times

Mexican Acorn Tortillas
Acorn Pemmican Tortilla
Acorn Bread and Acorn Muffins
Pioneer Acorn Pancakes
Breakfast Acorn meal (Similar to Oatmeal)
Acorn and Corn Meal Mush
Acorn Bread
Glazed Acorn Treats
Acorn Cookies
Chestnuts
Chestnut lasagne
Pasta
Pokeweed Casserole
Alfredo penne pasta
Croquettes
Turnovers

Dessert choices
Vanilla yogurt with walnuts
Ice cream and Jelly
Bread pudding
Fruit salad
Apple or berry pie
Brownies
Cakes and frosting

Snack choices
Chicken skin rinds
Hard baked bagels broken in pieces, sauced and seasoned
Seeds popped like popcorn
Dried seeds – sunflower / pumpkin / squash / fruit
Dried grapes for raisins and dried fruit
Nuts
Dried, seasoned vegetables
Potato chips
Nut brittle
Jerky

Chapter Seven:
Wild plant and
other categorized recipes

The author has received and tried many enjoyable recipes.
He has applied or modified various selections for improved
satisfaction and success.
Many of the recipes -
- Have been passed down from grandparents to their
  children and grandchildren.
- Are from indigenous tribal Indians.
- Come from descendants of early settlers and pioneers.

Hopefully in this book, the tastes of vegetarian and non-veg-
etarians will be satisfied.
Some of the suggested animals, birds and critters should
only be included in survival situations.

Disclaimer:
The recipes, methods and information presented herein
are intended for your reading pleasure. Experiencing success and enjoyment of the recipes may vary from person
to person. The writer and publisher makes no warranties,
expressed or implied, regarding the success, satisfaction and
accuracy of the recipes provided. The writer and publisher,
also assumes no legal or other liability and responsibility, for
any loss or injuries that may result from using the recipes or
information.
However every effort has been made to avoid errors, omissions and outdated or incorrect information.

Living in Difficult Times

In order to achieve success and complete satisfaction with the recipes, users may need to adjust the quantities or change the ingredients according to taste.

This may also be necessary because of gluten or other allergies or medical reasons.

Using the recipes and information in this book will constitute your acceptance of this disclaimer.

Canning fruit and vegetables for use during winter months could be very helpful.

How to make fresh fruit last longer during winter:
- Oranges and lemons
Refrigerate in a bowl of water
Change the water every week
They will remain hydrated for up to 3 months
- Apples
Remove all slightly spoiled apples.
Avoid washing them and handle them carefully to avoid bruising.
Wrap them individually in sheets of newspaper and place in a cardboard box.
Pack them tight enough to avoid air circulation.
They can be kept in an unheated basement, a pantry, an enclosed porch, an unheated attic or in a root cellar. Don't store them right next to potatoes.
They can be kept for several months.

How to make fresh vegetables last longer during winter:

- Cabbage
Late fall or winter cabbage may be stored for several months.
Pull out the cabbages with the roots and hang in a moist cellar.
or
Cut the heads and remove the loose outer leaves.
Place on a shelf as close to freezing as possible.

Chapter Seven: Wild plant and other categorized recipes

- Carrots
Cover in a container filled with damp (not wet) sand or garden soil and place in a cool dark place.
Carrots will keep fresh for months.

- Potatoes and onions
Use separate boxes for the potatoes and onions.
Fill each box with rice covering the potatoes or onions.
The rice will absorb moisture and keep the vegetables fresh.

- Beets
Leave about a half-inch of the stem and don't cut the root end to prevent bleeding.
Snip off the greens.
Lay them in layers of damp sand or sawdust, in a plastic container with a tight lid.

Suggested recipes

Teaspoon = tsp   Tablespoon = tbsp

Soups:

Soup or gravy thickener
Clean, grind and mix the following in the soup or gravy:
(add quantity for thickness)
- Sassafras leaves
- Slippery elm root
- Day lily flowers
- Cattail roots
- Kudzu roots
- Puréed rosehips

Remove the stems and burs from the rosehips.
Split them lengthwise and remove the seeds with a knife.
Place them in a pan with an equal amount of water.
Bring to a boil and simmer until they are softened.
After cooling, mash with a fork or blend with a blender.
The rosehip purée should be ready for use.

Raw blended vegetable soup
Ingredients:
- 1 carrot
- 1 celery stick
- 2 diced small tomatoes
- ½ potato cut in pieces
- ¼ yellow squash cut in pieces
- ¼ zucchini cut in pieces
- 2 cloves of garlic
- 1 diced mushroom
- ¼ Bell-pepper
- 6 cups of beef or vegetable broth
- ¼ cup of grated cheese
- 5 crushed corn chips
- Chilli powder and seasoning to taste

Preparation:
Blend in blender
Mix in ¼ can of pinto or kidney beans and serve cold or heat to serve warm

Pinto bean soup

   1 pound of pinto beans – boil and rinse
   Add 8 cups water
   Add one or two slices of ham, 1 diced carrot, 1 diced onion, 2 diced garlic cloves
   Salt and pepper to taste
   Slow cook for 4-8 hours
   Serves 6

Chicken noodle soup

Ingredients:
   8 cups chicken broth
   1 cup of spaghetti, or egg noodles or macaroni
   1 minced onion
   1 tsp of Italian herbs
   3 minced garlic cloves
   2 carrots diced
   1 cup celery diced
   2 to 3 cups cooked, diced chicken

Preparation:
Combine ingredients
Bring to a boil and simmer for 20 minutes
Serves 10

Cabbage soup

   ½ lb of ground beef or turkey
   Add
   1 tbsp of Paprika
   1 tsp of Allspice
   1 tsp of ground coriander seed
   Salt and pepper to taste

Preparation:
Brown the meat in oil and add a bay leaf
Place the browned meat in a pot
Add
1 cup diced tomatoes
1 diced onion and 2 diced garlic cloves
½ head of diced cabbage
5 to 6 cups of chicken stock
Cook for 30 minutes and serve with a sandwich

Dandelion soup
Sauté ½ cup of cut wild onions
Add 1 cup of mushrooms
Add 2 cups of dandelion leaves
Add 6 cups of beef or vegetable stock
Bring to a boil and simmer for 20 minutes
Serves 6

Burdock soup
Ingredients:
    6 cups of beef or vegetable stock
    2 cups of thinly sliced burdock root
    2 tbsp of vegetable oil
    6 cups of sliced mushrooms
    3 sliced celery stalks
    1 tbsp of fresh ginger
    4 cloves of chopped garlic
    ½ tsp of freshly ground anise seeds
    Salt and pepper to taste
    Add flour or milk to thicken (quantity according to thickness)

Preparation:
Place the stock and the sliced burdock root in a large pot
Simmer for 30 minutes
Heat the oil in a large skillet over medium heat
Add the mushrooms, celery, ginger, garlic and, stir for 10 minutes

Add it to the pot of boiling stock
Bring the pot to a boil over medium heat while stirring
Season
Add the thickener
Reduce to low and simmer for 10 minutes
Serves 6

Cream of mushroom soup

2 cups mushrooms sautéed in oiled pot with 1 diced onion
Add 5 cups of stock
Salt & pepper to taste
Add 1 cup of cream and simmer for 10 minutes to thicken
Serve

Watercress bisque

Ingredients:
2 tbsp of oil
1 tsp of ground mustard seed
4 cups watercress leaves
4 crushed cloves of garlic
½ tsp of tarragon
½ tsp of nutmeg
4 cups of vegetable stock
1 cup of cut potato pieces, simmered in water until tender and drained
Salt and pepper to taste

Preparation:
Heat the olive oil in a large skillet over medium heat
Add the ground mustard seeds and cook until the seeds pop
Stir in the watercress, garlic, tarragon, nutmeg, pepper and cook for 5 minutes
Blend in a blender
Add the remaining ingredients
Blend until smooth
Heat and serve

Living in Difficult Times

Watercress soup
Place 2 tbsp of olive oil in a skillet
Add 1 chopped Onion and sauté
Add 1 crushed clove of garlic
Add 1 thinly sliced Potato
Add 4 cups of chicken broth
Add 1 cup of Lambs Quarters (or Spinach)
Add 4 handfuls of watercress and sauté for 5 minutes

Place in a blender and blend
Then place in a pot and boil
Add 1 tbsp of cream
Salt and pepper to taste
Serve and garnish with some watercress leaves
Serves 6

Chanterelle mushroom soup
Ingredients:
 1½ lbs of chanterelle mushroom caps
 1 cup of chopped onion
 3 cloves of minced garlic
 ½ tsp of chilli powder
 7 tbsp of butter or olive oil
 1 tsp of ground black pepper
 1 tsp of salt
 7 cups of chicken broth
 1 cup of cream
 3 tbsp of chopped cilantro
 2 tbsp of flour
 ¼ cup of white wine

Preparation:
Heat a large skillet
Add butter and olive oil to the skillet
Add garlic, chanterelle caps, onions and leeks
Cook and stir for 3 minutes
Add white wine and stir
Cook for another 3 minutes
Remove from heat and set aside

80

Place chicken stock, chilli powder, salt and pepper in a pot and stir at medium heat
Pour in the chanterelle mixture and cook for 15 minutes
Allow it to cool, remove and blend in a blender
Return it to the pot
Separately whisk 2 tbsp of flour with 1 cup of cream and stir in a bowl
Pour it into the pot and bring to a boil
Cook for about 4 minutes until it thickens
Serve

Amaranth soup
    3 cups of amaranth greens boiled in 6 cups of broth
    Add 2 beaten eggs
    Add ½ cup of cream
    Add salt & pepper to taste
    Simmer for 6 minutes and serve

Stinging nettle soup
Ingredients:
    1 lb of stinging nettle leaves
    7 cups water
    1 cup of nuts, soaked in water overnight
    2 tbsp of oil
    ½ tsp of nutmeg
    1 tbsp of lemon juice
    Salt and pepper to taste
    One chopped medium onion

Preparation:
Sauté the onion in oil until it is translucent
Blend (in a blender) the nettle leaves in six cups of water and add to a pot
Blend nuts with a cup of water and add to pot
Add the nutmeg and lemon juice
Salt and pepper to taste
Simmer for 20 minutes
Serve

Wild onion soup
Sauté 4 cups of sliced wild onions
Add 6 cups vegetable or chicken broth and simmer until soft
Add ½ cup of butter and 2 crushed cloves of garlic
Season to taste
Simmer for 10 minutes
Serve

Cream of Asparagus soup
Sauté 4 cups of sliced asparagus
Add 6 cups vegetable or chicken broth and simmer until
  soft
Add 1 cup cream and 2 crushed cloves of garlic
Season to taste
Simmer for 10 minutes
Serve

Sheep sorrel soup
Boil 6 cups of vegetable or chicken broth
Add 5 cups of uncooked sorrel leaves
Add ½ cup of sautéed onions
Add salt, pepper and nutmeg to taste
Add 2 medium thinly sliced potatoes
Simmer for 30 minutes
Serve

Curly Dock soup
Ingredients:
4 cups of chopped curly dock leaves
1 cup of diced onion
2 tbsp of olive oil
4 large sliced potatoes
6 cups of water
Salt and pepper to taste
3 cups of milk, yogurt, or cream

Preparation:
Sauté the onion in olive oil until it is translucent
Add curly dock leaves and cook
Stir until the green colour lightens
Add the potatoes and water
Boil the potatoes until they are soft
Season to taste
Blend with a blender
Serve

Hickory nut soup
Grind the Hickory nuts until they are fine
Form them into balls that are three inches in diameter
Place them in a fridge or freezer
Boil 8 of the balls in a pan with 6 cups of water
Once dissolved, simmer until it has a creamlike texture
Add sugar or honey to taste
Serve

Turtle soup
Ingredients:
Soak 2 pounds of fresh turtle meat in vinegar for 30 minutes
8 cups water
2 sliced green onions
1 sliced celery stalk
1 large finely chopped onion
1 crushed garlic clove
1 tbsp of finely chopped parsley
5 tbsp of butter
2 tbsp of flour
½ cup of tomatoes
Salt and pepper to taste

Preparation:
Place the turtle meat in the water
Add the salt, pepper, green onions, celery and boil for 1 hour

Remove the foam regularly from the top to create a clear broth
Strain out the broth and keep it for later use
Set the turtle meat aside
In a large pot mix the flour and butter to make a brown roux
Add the onion, parsley, garlic and tomatoes
Simmer over a low heat for approximately 10 minutes
Add the turtle meat and broth
Then simmer for approximately 2 hours, until the meat is tender
Season with salt and pepper to taste
Add Vinegar to taste if desired
Serve

Salads
Use a combination of any salad greens
or
Use salad greens mixed together with vegetables or vegetable substitutes
Nuts may be added
Flower petals may be added – (Like evening primrose, white magnolia, rose)

Shepherds purse salad
Ingredients:
   4 cups of chopped shepherd's purse (or other greens)
   1 cup of sliced potatoes
   ½ cup of parsley or cilantro
   1½ cups of oil
   Juice of 1 lemon
   2 cloves of garlic
   1 tsp of fresh ginger
   1 tsp of rosemary
   1 tsp of turmeric
   Salt and pepper

Preparation of the dressing:
Place 1½ cups of vegetable oil in a blender
Add the lemon juice

Add 1 cup of water
Add the other ingredients
Salt and pepper to taste
Blend until smooth
Now toss the shepherd's purse salad with the dressing
Serve.

Carrot, Yam or Sweet potato salad
Grate the required amount of carrots, yams or sweet potato
Add orange juice and seasonings to taste
Serve

Cold slaw
Ingredients:
    Set aside 6 cups of shredded Cabbage or Amaranth
    1 grated medium yam or sweet potato
    Ingredients:
    2 tbsp of sugar (to taste)
    4 tbsp of vinegar
    Salt & pepper to taste
    3 tbsp of mayonnaise

Preparation:
Mix the greens, yam or sweet potato
Separately mix the sugar, vinegar, salt, pepper and then add the mayonnaise
Pour it over the shredded greens, mix and serve

Fruit salad
Any combination of sliced fruit mixed with a selected fruit juice

Salad Dressings:

Honey mustard dressing
Ingredients:
    1/3 cup of honey
    ¼ cup of mustard
    ¼ cup of cider vinegar

2 tbsp of lemon juice
1 minced garlic clove
1 cup of vegetable oil

Preparation:
Blend the ingredients (not the oil)
Gradually add the oil until it has a smooth and creamy texture
Keep in a refrigerator and shake well before using

Poppy seed dressing
Ingredients:
1 cup of sugar
3 tsp of ground mustard
Salt and pepper to taste
2/3 cup of vinegar
¼ cup of chopped onion
2 cups of olive oil
2 tbsp of poppy seeds

Preparation:
Blend the sugar, mustard, salt, vinegar, and onion in a blender
Add vegetable oil slowly until the dressing is smooth and has a creamy texture
Add poppy seeds and blend
Cover and keep in a refrigerator
Shake well before using

Caesar salad dressing
Ingredients:
1½ cups of vegetable Oil
¾ cup of fresh orange juice
¼ cup of fresh lemon juice
3 tbsp of grated parmesan cheese
3 cloves of garlic
Salt and pepper to taste

Preparation:
Blend all ingredients in blender until smooth
Cover and refrigerate
Shake well before using

Italian dressing
    ½ cup of vinegar
    2 tbsp of vegetable oil
    Add salt & pepper to taste
    Keep in a refrigerator
    Shake well before using

Ranch salad dressing
Ingredients:
    ¾ cup of mayonnaise
    ¾ cup of buttermilk
    1 tbsp of finely chopped celery leaves
    1 tbsp of finely chopped green onions
    1 tbsp of finely chopped fresh parsley
    3 tsp of fresh lemon juice
    3 tsp of minced garlic
    Salt and pepper to taste

Preparation:
Mix the garlic, mayonnaise and buttermilk
Add the celery leaves, green onions, parsley, lemon juice, black pepper and salt
Stir to blend
Keep in a refrigerator
Shake well before using

Greens
Select any combination of mixed greens -
    Young and tender new poke leaves (in April)
    Lamb's Quarters
    Dandelion
    Curly Dock
    Watercress
    and
    5 pieces of bacon (From hog or wild boar)
    2 tbsp of sugar
    3 tbsp of vinegar

Living in Difficult Times

Preparation:
Steam the cut greens until they are soft
Fry bacon in a separate skillet until crisp and then remove
Pour vinegar and sugar into the skillet and stir
Add the broken pieces of bacon and the greens, a little at a time and stir
Cover reducing the heat, simmer and serve

Choose any combination of mixed greens
>   Stinging nettle / Amaranth / Chickweed
>   Lambs quarters / Water cress
>   Sochan (young top leaves)
>   Wild mustard greens (spring)
>   Duckweed – found floating on ponds (must clean thoroughly)
>   Dock (young and tender leaves)
>   Sorrel leaves
>   Solomon seal (young leaves)
>   and
>   Wild onions
>   Salt & pepper to taste

Preparation:
Boil greens in a pot and rinse
Heat vegetable oil in a skillet
Add the boiled greens
Salt, pepper and season to taste
Fry until done and serve

Sautéed Greens
Ingredients:
>   5 cups of chopped greens
>   3 cups of chopped onions
>   4 tablespoons of vegetable oil
>   2 cups of grated carrots
>   1 tbsp of soy sauce
>   1 tbsp of wine
>   3 minced cloves of garlic
>   Salt and pepper to taste

Preparation:
Sauté the onions in oil
When soft, add the carrots, greens, garlic, wine and soy sauce
Cook for 20 minutes
Serve

Collard greens
    Sauté 3 garlic cloves and 3 chopped onions in cooking oil
    Add 6 cups collard greens
    Add 6 cups of boiling chicken broth
    Add some pieces of Ham
    Salt, pepper and season to taste
    Simmer for 2 hours
    Serve when tender

Purslane
    Toast a cup of crushed nuts
    Add 5 spoons of bacon grease
    When it sizzles stir in the 6 cups of purslane greens
    Reduce the heat and continue stirring until the purslane is wilted
    Remove and serve.

Blue Violet
    Use the fresh young leaves in salads or cook as greens
    They are high in both vitamins A and C

Amaranth greens
    Place 6 cups of amaranth greens in a pot
    Add 1 cup of young mustard greens or dandelion greens
    Add salt and pepper to taste
    Cook lightly and drain
    Sauté with onions and bacon

Chickweed
    Place 6 cups of chickweed leaves and stems in a pot
    Add 2 cups of wild onions
    Add 1 cup of Water cress
    Salt & pepper to taste
    Cook, drain and serve with butter

Curried Greens
Ingredients:
    4 tbsp of oil
    9 cups of young dandelion leaves or other greens
    5 chopped garlic cloves
    2 cups of water
    2 tbsp of flour
    1 cup of milk
    Salt and pepper to taste
    2 tbsp of curry powder

Preparation:
Sauté the dandelion leaves and garlic in the oil for about 8 minutes
Blend the remaining ingredients in a blender
Add it to the dandelions and bring to a boil
Reduce the heat to low, cover, simmer 8 minutes
Serve

Sautéed Ramps
    1 lb of meat
    ½ cup of vegetable oil
    20 small wild onions or 3 onions (Chopped)
    4 cloves of crushed garlic
    ½ tsp of turmeric
    Sage, nutmeg and cilantro to taste
    ¼ cup of milk
    ¼ cup of wine

Preparation:
Sauté the meat in a large frying pan with oil
Add the ramps (onions) and ½ tsp of turmeric
Heat over medium heat for 6 minutes, stirring often
Add the garlic and sauté another 3 minutes
Add the milk, wine, sage, nutmeg, cilantro
Cover and cook for 20 minutes
Serve

Other lunch or dinner choices

Sautéed Cactus leaves with Peppers and Corn
Ingredients:
    4 large bell peppers (red or green)
    1 large onion
    2 tbsp of butter
    4 cups of corn
    1 lb of edible peeled cactus cut into ½ inch pieces
    Cilantro or parsley to taste

Preparation:
Cut the peppers into ½ inch squares
Dice the onions
Place them in a skillet and cook over moderate heat until soft
Add the cactus and corn
Stir over high heat for about 6 minutes
Salt and pepper to taste and add cilantro or parsley
Serve hot

Seven different ways to use potatoes or their substitutes:

1. Slice and serve them raw along with snacks and dips
2. Shred them raw into a slaw
3. Cook and slice them into a potato salad
4. Chop and blend them with other vegetables when preparing soups
6. Make fries and fry them in cooking oil
6. Boil and mash them as mashed potatoes
7. Use as mashed potato in a cottage pie

Curried Potatoes
Ingredients:
    6 Potatoes (medium size)
    3 Large onions
    3 crushed Garlic gloves
    1 can of diced tomatoes
    1 to 2 tbsp of mild curry powder to taste
    1 tbsp of vegetable oil
    1 tsp of coriander seed
    Salt and pepper to taste

Preparation:
Dice the onions and fry them with the garlic in a pot
Cut the potatoes in quarters and add to the onions
Mix in the curry powder
Add the tomatoes on top of the potatoes
Add the coriander and cover
Simmer at low heat for about 70 minutes
Salt and pepper to taste
Serve

Other potato substitute preparations:
Daylily tubers
They are crisper and sweeter than potatoes
They may be used similarly to regular potatoes

Arrowhead tubers
They are white, egg-shaped and about the size of a golf ball
They may be boiled for 30 minutes or roasted in campfire embers and then peeled

Jerusalem artichoke
Jerusalem Artichokes have small, starchy tubers on the roots
They may be eaten raw, added to salads, or cooked as potatoes
They are crisp and sweet especially after the first frost

They may be used in the following ways:
- Slice, dice, or stir fry them along with other fresh vegetables in oil

- Baked whole or sliced
Toss them in a bowl with a little oil and place on a baking sheet
Bake them in an oven temperature at 375° F for about 20 minutes, turning them half way through.
Season with salt and pepper to taste

- Steamed
Cut the Jerusalem artichokes in halves and steam them for 10 minutes
Season them to taste

Chapter Seven: Wild plant and other categorized recipes

- Boiled
Boil the Jerusalem artichokes tubers for 30 minutes
Season and serve whole or as mashed potatoes

- Combination baked
Ingredients:
    1 lb of sliced Jerusalem artichokes tubers
    2 cups of tomato sauce
    3 tbsp of cooking oil
    2 tbsp of fresh parsley
    2 tbsp of lemon juice
    ½ tsp of tarragon
    Sugar or honey to taste
    2 tbsp of chopped parsley
    3 tbsp of toasted ground nuts

Preparation:
Mix all ingredients (except the parsley and nuts)
Marinate, cover and refrigerate overnight
Drain and bake uncovered at 350° F in a shallow baking sheet for 35 minutes
Garnish with parsley and nuts
Serve

Jerusalem Artichoke Casserole
Ingredients:
    4 cups of cooked, mashed Jerusalem artichokes
    2 cups of bread crumbs
    ½ cup of cooking oil
    2 beaten eggs

Preparation:
Place the cooked Jerusalem Artichokes in a bowl
Mix in the bread crumbs
Mix in the oil
Mix in the eggs
Season with salt and pepper to taste
Place the mixture in a casserole dish
Bake in an oven at 350° F for about 30 minutes
Garnish the top according to taste (bread crumbs and cheese)
Serves 8

Chips
Jerusalem Artichokes or potatoes
    - Baked chips:
Cut them into thin chip slices (1/8 of inch)
Sprinkle with oil
Sprinkle with salt and seasoning to taste
Pre-heat the oven to 400° F
Evenly space the chips on a baking sheet
Bake and flip them over after about 7 minutes
Bake for another 7 minutes or until they are golden brown
Take them out of the oven, let them cool and serve

    - Deep Fried chips:
Pour oil into a deep frying pan or pot and heat to 350° F
Do not overfill the pan with oil as it will rise when boiling
Add several slices at a time
Submerge and fries in the oil until chips are firm and browned
Remove the chips and let them dry out on a paper towel
Salt and season to taste
Serve

- Groundnut tubers:
Slice the tubers, fry or cook with bacon and onions

Dandelions
Dandelion buds
Pick unopened buds very close to the stem
Put them in a cupful of cold water with 1 teaspoons of salt for fifteen minutes
Drain and place them in water in a covered pan and bring them to a boil
Lower the heat and simmer for 15 minutes
Drain the excess liquid and serve with butter
Season to taste

Chapter Seven: Wild plant and other categorized recipes

Dandelion fritters
Ingredients:
    Pick fully opened blossoms
    Trim the stems very close to the heads
    Soak them in cold salt water for three hours and rinse in cold running water

Preparation:
Roll the blossoms in egg and dip them in flour
Roll the floured blossoms in egg again
Then dip them again in flour
Fry them in hot oil in a pan until they are golden brown
Drain and serve them

Milkweed pods
Pick milkweed pods less than 1 inch in length
(Larger pods will cause an upset stomach)
Place the pods in a pot and cover them with boiling water
Continue cooking for 5 minutes and pour off the water
Again pour fresh boiling water over the pods and boil for 5 minutes
Pour off the water and again pour fresh boiling water over the pods
Boil for 15 minutes
Pour off the water and serve the pods with butter
Salt and pepper to taste

Wild onions
Use just like regular onions

Mushroom types:
    Wine cap
    Prince
    Dryad saddle
    Morel
    Oyster
    Puff ball
    Meadow

Chanterelle
Bolette
Horse
Shaggy parasol

Mushroom recipes:

Chanterelle mushroom lasagne
Ingredients:
3 lbs of sliced chanterelle mushrooms
2 lbs of sliced other mushrooms
5 tbsp of butter
4 medium sliced onions
4 crushed cloves of garlic
2 tbsp of fresh sage
1 cup of heavy cream
Salt and black pepper to taste
Nutmeg to taste
3 or more sheets of pasta, 10" square
(or smaller pieces to cover the same area)
4 cups of grated mozzarella cheese
2 cups of grated parmesan cheese

Preparation:
Melt 4 tbsp of butter over medium heat in a large skillet
Add the mushrooms
Sauté for a few minutes
Add the sliced onions, garlic, sage and sauté for three minutes
Add the cream and simmer
Cook until it thickens
Season with salt, pepper and nutmeg
Place the mixture in a bowl for later use
Boil a large pot of water
Add the pasta sheets for just two minutes and drain into a colander
Butter a lasagne pan with the remaining butter
Place the first layer of pasta sheets on the bottom of the pan
Pour half of the mushroom mixture evenly over it

Cover it with ½ of the parmesan and ¼ of the mozzarella cheese
Add a second layer of pasta sheets
Pour the other half of the mushroom mixture evenly over it
Cover it with the other ½ of the parmesan and ¼ of the mozzarella cheese
Add the third layer of pasta sheets
Arrange the sage leaves over it and add the remaining mozzarella on top
Cover with aluminium foil and bake at 325° F for 30 minutes
Take it out of the oven and remove the aluminium foil
Then broil it until it is brown
Let it rest for 10 minutes
Sprinkle the remaining ¼ of parmesan cheese on the top
Serve

Wild Mushroom Pasta Primavera
Ingredients:
    1 lb of Mushrooms
    1 lb of dried pasta
    ½ cup of grated cheese
    ¾ cup of white wine
    4 cloves of chopped garlic
    1 tsp of thyme
    Salt & Pepper to taste

Preparation:
Boil the pasta for 8 minutes and drain
Simmer the mushrooms in wine in a separate pot
Add the thyme and garlic
Add the cooked pasta to the mushrooms
Season with salt and pepper to taste
Stir in the cheese
Serve

Wild Mushroom Bread Serving
Ingredients:
- 4 tbsp of vegetable oil
- 1 cup of sliced onions
- 1 lb of mixed wild mushrooms
- 3 tsp of minced garlic
- Salt and black pepper to taste
- 6 eggs
- 3 cups of heavy cream
- ½ cup of honey
- 2 tsp of Worcestershire sauce (see recipe)
- 1 tsp of minced fresh thyme leaves
- 2 cups of freshly grated Cheddar cheese
- 11 cups of bread, cut into 1 inch cubes
- 2 tbsp of butter
- 1 cup of dried bread crumbs

Preparation:
Heat the oil over high heat in a large skillet
Add the onions and cook until brown and tender
Add the mushrooms and garlic
Salt and pepper to taste
Cook and stir until the mushrooms are tender for about 6 minutes
Keep stirring until the mixture is almost dry
Remove from the heat and let it cool

In a bowl, combine eggs, cream and honey
Then add the Worcestershire sauce and thyme
Salt and pepper to taste
Blend
Add the cheese and stir
Add the bread cubes and wait for about 2 hours to absorb the liquid

Preheat the oven to 350° F
Butter a baking dish
Add the bread crumbs covering the bottom evenly

Pour the bread pudding mixture over it and cover with aluminium foil
Bake for 1 hour and then uncover it
Then continue baking for about 35 minutes until it rises and is browned
Let it cool
Serve

Morel Quiche
Ingredients:
    1 lb of morel mushrooms
    ½ lb of bacon
    ½ Cup of chopped onions
    ½ Cup of chopped green peppers
    1½ Cups of shredded Swiss cheese
    2 Cups of milk
    1 Cup of Bisquick
    3 Eggs
    Salt and pepper to taste

Preparation:
Sauté the bacon and morel mushrooms in a skillet with oil
Add and sauté the onion and green pepper
Preheat oven to 400° F
Coat a 10 inch oven dish with butter
Add the sautéed mushrooms and mix in the cheese in the oven dish
Mix in the milk, eggs, bisquick, salt, pepper and stir until smooth
Bake for 40 minutes
Test it by inserting a toothpick and if it comes out clean, it is done
Serve

Grilled Portobello Mushroom Steaks
Ingredients:
   6 large Portobello mushroom caps
   ½ of cup cooking oil
   ½ cup of white wine
   Juice of 1 lemon
   2 minced cloves of garlic
   Salt and pepper to taste

Preparation:
Remove the stems of the mushrooms and clean
Combine in a bowl the oil, wine, lemon juice and garlic to use as a marinade
Submerge the mushroom caps in the marinade for 45 minutes
Remove from the marinade
Salt and pepper to taste
Grill the caps over medium heat for 4 minutes per side, until tender
Serve

Mushroom burger
   Brush a large Mushroom cap (Like Shitake)with oil and grill for 3 minutes
   Turn them over and grill for another 3 minutes
   Fill with Shredded lettuce or greens and add a slice of tomato and onion
   Add mustard and condiments
   Serve

Chilli stuffed mushrooms
Ingredients:
   6 large Portobello mushroom caps
   4 tbsp of oil
   10 oz of chopped bacon
   1 medium finely chopped bell pepper
   ½ cup of breadcrumbs
   ½ cup of corn kernels
   2 sheets of foil

Preparation:
Heat 1 tbsp of oil in a pan
Fry bacon and bell pepper for three minutes
Pour into a bowl, add and mix in the remaining ingredients
Place the 1st foil inside a baking sheet and lightly spread butter over it
Arrange the 6 mushroom caps on the foil
Fill each mushroom with the ingredients
Cover the mushrooms and baking sheet with 2nd foil
Bake in an oven at 375º F, for about twelve minutes
Serve with toast

Trout / shitake mushrooms / tomatoes and ginger
Ingredients:
- 4 whole gutted rainbow trout
- 4 chopped green onions
- 4 large fresh shiitake mushrooms, stemmed, and the caps thinly sliced
- 1 cup of chopped tomatoes
- 4 teaspoons of minced fresh ginger
- 4 minced garlic cloves
- 8 tsp of soy sauce
- 4 tsp of cooking oil
- Cilantro to taste

Preparation:
Preheat oven to 400°F
Place foil in a baking sheet and spread it with butter
Open each fish like a book, skin side down on the foil
Salt and pepper the fish to taste
Mix the ingredients and sprinkle over the fish
Drizzle the soy sauce and oil over it and top it with the cilantro
Bake uncovered for up to 24 minutes until the fish is done and serve

Potato Nests with sautéed Mushrooms

For each potato nest (Adjust according to the size of the wire baskets)
3 large potatoes
Cooking oil for deep-frying the nests
A larger and smaller wire basket that fit into each other
Salt and pepper to taste

Make the potato nests. (As many as you need)
Place the peeled potatoes in a bowl of ice water for 5 minutes
Then take them out and grate them coarsely
Replace them in a bowl of water
Drain them in a colander and pat them dry
Heat the oil to 375°F in a deep fryer
(Do not overfill the deep fryer with oil as it may boil over)

Dip the larger wire basket into the hot oil of the fryer and remove it
Then line the bottom and side with some grated potatoes, *(don't burn your fingers)*
Dip the smaller wire basket into the hot oil
Then press it into the larger potato-lined basket and press them firmly together
Place both into the oil and fry the potato nest for 3 minutes, until golden crisp
Remove from the oil and detach the smaller basket out of the larger one
Let the potato nest cool in the smaller basket for 5 minutes
Insert a sharp knife tip between the wires to loosen the nest
Remove the potato nest carefully from the smaller basket and do not break it
Keep warm
Place the mushroom mixture in the potato nests and serve

Mushroom mixture (More may be needed for larger baskets)
½ cup butter
1 pound of thinly sliced shitake or other mushrooms
½ cup of wine (good tasting)
4 tablespoons of heavy cream
2 tablespoons of finely chopped parsley leaves

How to make the mushroom mixture:
Heat butter in a skillet at medium heat
Add and sauté the mushrooms until they are tender
Stir in the wine until it evaporates and then stir in the cream
Add the parsley, salt and pepper to taste

Meats

Meat dishes grilled, stewed or curried

Kebabs – 2 inch cubes of meat alternated on skewers with fruit pieces or vegetables

Meatloaf
Ingredients:
   3 cups of ground meat (or 3 cans of pinto beans for vegetarian)
   1 cup of mushrooms
   2 onions
   2 sliced tomatoes
   ½ cup of bread crumbs
   2 tsp of vegetable oil
   2 beaten eggs
   2 cloves of garlic
   Salt and pepper to taste

Preparation:
Preheat the oven to 400° F
Mix the tomato and meat (or pinto beans) in a bowl
Add the dry ingredients
Add and mix the oil, eggs, garlic, salt, pepper
Place it into a greased loaf pan
Bake for about 20 minutes in the preheated oven
Top it with tomato sauce and bake another 15 minutes until firm
Serve

Hamburger sausage
Ingredients:
- 2 lbs of ground meat (Beef, deer or turkey)
- 1 lb of bread crumbs
- 4 beaten eggs
- 1 cup of wild onions
- Salt, pepper and seasoning to taste

Preparation:
Mix all the ingredients
Shape into hand-size balls and flatten them into burgers
or
Stuff in casings to make Italian sausage or bratwurst
or
Use to make a meatloaf

Vegetarian hamburger sausage – (without meat)
Ingredients:
- 1 lb of kidney beans
- 1 lb of black beans
- 1 lb of bread crumbs
- 2 cups of greens
- 1 cup of mixed vegetables
- 4 beaten eggs
- 1 cup of diced onions or wild onions
- Salt, pepper and seasoning to taste

Preparation:
Mix all the ingredients
Shape into hand-size balls and flatten them into burgers
or
Stuff in casings to make Italian sausage or bratwurst
or
Use to make a meatloaf

Veggie burger –without meat
Ingredients:
- 1 cup of kidney beans
- 1 cup of black beans
- 1 cup of bread crumbs or rolled oats
- ½ cup of grated carrots

2 cups of greens
1 cup of mixed vegetables
3 minced garlic cloves
3 beaten eggs
¾ cup of diced onions or wild onions
Salt, pepper to taste

Preparation:
Mix all the ingredients
Divide and shape into hand-size balls and then flatten each one into a burger
Refrigerate for 2 hours
Then lightly coat each side of the burger with flour
Cook in a lightly oiled skillet on each side for about 4 minutes until slightly brown
Serve on a bun with the trimmings
Enjoy

Italian Sausage
Ingredients:
5 lbs of ground pork
2 tbsp of salt
Pepper to taste
1 tbsp of cracked fennel seed
½ tbsp of ground coriander
1½ tbsp of paprika
½ cup of sugar
½ cup of water

Preparation:
Combine the ground meat with the all ingredients and mix well
Stuff into hog or collagen casings with a ¾" sausage tube
Use 22-26 mm casings to make breakfast sausage links
Use 32-36 mm casings to make Italian and bratwurst links
Be careful as they will burst if stuffed too full, when you begin to form the links
To form the links, press the forefinger and thumb of the one hand together over the stuffed casing every 6 inches
Where you do that, twist it with the other hand 3 turns
For the next link repeat the process, twisting the link in the opposite direction

Complete the process making the needed amount of links
Bake, fry or grill
Serve.

Shepherd's pie
Ingredients:
> 2 cups of ground beef (or chicken or cooked lentils)
> ½ cup of diced mushrooms
> 1 cup of peas
> 1 diced stalk of celery
> 1 diced carrot
> 2 lbs of cooked mashed potatoes
> 1 diced onion
> 1 cup of milk
> 2 tbsp of cream
> 3 minced cloves of garlic
> 2 tbsp of flour
> 2 cups of beef broth
> 1 tbsp of Worcestershire sauce
> Salt and pepper to taste

Preparation:
Cook the potatoes for 25 minutes
Drain and mash with butter, milk or cream
Salt and pepper to taste
Cook the meat in a skillet for 8 minutes
Add the carrots, celery, mushrooms, garlic and sauté for 10 minutes
Sprinkle with flour and stir for 2 minutes
Stir in the broth, Worcestershire sauce and simmer for 10 minutes
Pour into a baking dish, add and mix in the peas
Season with salt and pepper
Spread the mashed potatoes over it
Bake in an oven at 350° F for 30 minutes
Then broil for 2 minutes until the top is golden
Serve

Chicken

May be fried, grilled or rottiserated
May be stewed with vegetables
May be curried with vegetables
May be cubed as kebabs on skewers with alternate vegetables and fruit, then grilled

Fried Chicken (similar to Kentucky)
Ingredients:
    1 chicken cut into pieces
    1 teaspoon of chopped tarragon
    1 tsp of chopped chives
    1 tsp of chopped parsley
    2 minced cloves of garlic
    1 tsp of cayenne pepper
    1 beaten egg
    1 cup of flour
    Salt & pepper to taste
    Oil to fry the chicken

Preparation:
Mix the chicken with salt, pepper, spices, garlic, chilli, egg and 2 tbsp of water
Coat chicken with flour and it must stick to the chicken (Add more water or flour if needed)
Heat the oil to 350° F in a skillet and slowly add the chicken pieces
Reduce heat to medium and cook in the covered skillet for 6 minutes
Turn the chicken and continue to cook for another 6 minutes
Ensure that both sides are golden brown and if necessary turn the chicken
Place the chicken pieces on a paper towel to drain the oil
Serve

Watercress stuffed chicken breasts
Ingredients:
   4 cups of watercress
   ½ lb of cream cheese

Preparation:
Blend the watercress and cream cheese in a blender
Flatten 4 chicken breasts – to ½ inch thick
Divide the watercress mixture into 4 parts
Place each part in the middle of a raw chicken breast
Fold and close the breasts
Place on a flat roasting pan
Brush each piece with olive oil
Bake at 250° F in the oven for about 20 to 30 minutes
Serve

Chicken and dumplings
Ingredients:
   For the stew -
   ½ cup of flour
   2lbs of 1½ inch cut chicken pieces
   1 cup of peas
   2 stalks of sliced celery
   2 sliced carrots
   2 sliced onions
   2 crushed garlic cloves
   ½ tsp of thyme
   1 tsp of sage
   Salt and pepper to taste
   4 cups of chicken broth
   2 tbsp of cooking oil
   ½ cup of cream

   For the dumplings -
   1½ cups of flour
   ½ tsp of baking soda
   ¼ tsp of salt
   1¼ cups of buttermilk

Preparation:
For the stew -
Toss and cover the chicken in a bag with flour, thyme, sage, salt and pepper
Heat the oil in a skillet
Add the chicken and brown for about 8 minutes on all sides
Add the onions and garlic and sauté for 3 minutes
Add the carrots, celery and sauté for 5 minutes
Sprinkle with the flour that's left over in the bag and sauté for 3 minutes
Add the chicken broth and simmer for 10 minutes
Stir in the cream and simmer for 5 minutes

For the dumplings -
Mix the flour, salt and baking soda
Mix in the buttermilk to form sticky dough and set aside for 3 minutes

Add the peas to the stew
Then drop in spoon size sticky dough amounts into the stew
Cook for 15 minutes
Serve

Turkey
May be fried, grilled or rottiserated
May be stewed with vegetables
May be curried with vegetables
May be cubed as kebabs on skewers with alternate vegetables and fruit, then grilled

Chicken / Turkey pie
Ingredients:
2 cups of diced or cubed, cooked chicken or turkey pieces
1 cup of sliced mushrooms
1 cup of frozen peas
1 cup of mixed vegetables
1 cup of chopped onions
1 cup of cream of mushroom soup
Salt and pepper to taste

Living in Difficult Times

Preparation:
Make the flattened pie crust dough

Pie crust
2½ cups of flour
½ tsp of salt
1 cup of margarine
1/3 cup of cold water

Preparation:
Mix the flour and salt in large bowl
Blend 2/3 of a cup of margarine into the flour
The mixture should have a texture like cornmeal
Add the rest of the margarine until it crumbs the size of peas
Sprinkle 1 tbsp of water at a time, over the mixture
Toss it with a fork until the particles stick together
(Using too much water will make the pie crust dough sticky and the pastry tough.
Too little water will make the dough crumbly and hard to work with)
Gently form a ball by pressing the particles together
Wrap it in plastic and refrigerate for 45 minutes
Then divide the ball of dough in half
(One half for the bottom pie crust and the other for the top)
Then sprinkle a flat work surface lightly with flour
Flatten the first half of the dough gently and sprinkle the top with flour
Rub some flour onto a rolling pin
Roll out the dough from the centre to the edge in all directions
Roll it out to form a circle about 2" wider than the size of the pie pan
Turn the pie crust dough around a few times while rolling it out
Make sure that it isn't sticking to the work surface
If necessary, dust it again with flour
Make the second ball of dough similarly for the top of the pie
Finish making the pie:
Fold the first flattened pie crust dough in half, then in half again to form a 1/4 circle

Unfold and ease it into a pan that has been lightly buttered
It should cover the bottom and sides of the pan
Prick some holes in it with a fork
Bake it for about 5 minutes until it is slightly brown
Fill it with the ingredients (but not the mushroom soup or salt and pepper)
Then pour over the mushroom soup
Then salt and pepper to taste
Cover the ingredients with the second pie crust
Wet the edge all around the side and press the crusts together with a fork
Make two small slits in the top crust
Bake at 350° F for 30 minutes or until brown and serve

Other Bird

Choose any of the following - Pheasant / Grouse / Quail / Duck / Partridge / Geese
   1 dressed bird
   A mixture of the following Vegetable Stuffing to be placed
      in the bird:
   1 cup of finely chopped onion
   3 tbsp of butter or margarine
   1 cup of coarsely grated carrots
   ¾ cup of finely diced celery
   2 tbsp of chopped parsley
   Salt and pepper to taste

Dough Blanket to cover the bird:
   Ingredients:
   2 cups of flour
   1 tsp of salt
   2 tbsp of margarine
   ½ cup of water

Preparation:
Mix the dry ingredients
Then mix in the water
Gently form the soft dough mixture into a ball
Wrap the ball in plastic and refrigerate for 45 minutes

Now rinse the bird inside and outside with warm water and
drain
Sauté the onions in an oiled skillet and then add the veg-
etables and seasonings
Place the mixture into the cavity of the bird
Roll out the dough ball on a lightly floured surface
Roll it into a sheet about 18 inches square
Wrap the dough around bird, completely covering it
Moisten the edges and pinch them together to seal
Place in a roasting pan
Roast in an oven, uncovered at 350° F for up to 2 hours
Use the drippings for gravy
Break off the crusty brown blanket in pieces and serve it
with the bird and gravy

Roasted duck

Preheat the oven to 375°F
Place the duck on a clean carving board
Remove excess fat from the neck and body cavity
Rinse the duck with cold water inside and outside and
pat dry
Pierce the skin of the duck all over at 2 inch spacing
Rub salt and pepper all over the duck (or other season-
ings desired)
Place the duck, breast side up in a roasting pan
Pour 2 cups of boiling water over the duck
Roast the duck for up to 3 hours until the skin is crisp
and brown
Turn the duck over every 30 minutes
Each time baste the duck with orange, apple or pine-
apple juice when turning
When done, remove it from the oven onto a carving
board
Let it rest for 15 minutes before carving and serving

Diced marinated duck
Ingredients:
- 6 cups of diced duck
- 3 sliced onions
- 6 pureed plums
- 4 sliced plums
- Soy sauce to taste
- 3 cups of water
- Cooking Oil
- Salt and pepper to taste

Preparation:
Make a marinade with the onion, plums, soy sauce, olive oil and water in a bowl
Add the diced duck and allow marinating for 50 minutes
Remove the duck pieces and fry them in a little oil (keep the marinade)
When browned, remove the duck from the pan
Add the kept marinade mixture back in the pan
Bring to a boil and immediately reduce the heat and simmer for 8 minutes
Add the 4 plums to the pan with the fried duck
Stir and cook for 5 more minutes
Serve

Curried duck
Ingredients:
- 6 cups of diced duck meat
- 3 sliced onions
- 6 pears
- 3 peaches
- 3 sliced potatoes
- Ground cumin, turmeric, chilli powder and ginger (½ tsp of each)
- 2 tbsp of curry powder
- 3 tbsp of Cooking Oil
- 3 cups of water
- Salt and pepper to taste

Living in Difficult Times

Preparation:
Mix together the spices
Slice the onions and set aside
Cut the pears and peaches into 1½ inch pieces and set
aside
Slice the skinless duck meat, season and set it aside
Heat oil in a pan and stir in the spices
Add and stir in the onions
Reduce the heat and cook until the onions are soft
Add the pear, peach pieces and water to the pan
Bring it to the boil and stir for three minutes
Reduce the heat and add the sliced potato
Add the seasoning and curry
Add the salt and pepper to taste
Cover and simmer until the curried fruit chunks are tender
While doing that fry the duck pieces in a pan sepately in oil
until browned
Remove the pan from the heat
Allow the meat to rest for 5 minutes
Pour the curried fruit chunks that are tender into a platter
Mix in the meat with the curried fruit on the platter and
serve with rice

Pigeon
Place the slightly salted pieces of meat in a bag containing ½
cup of flour
Shake the bag to coat the meat well
Melt a quarter pound of butter in a pan and fry the pigeon at
very low heat
When it is golden brown remove, allow to rest for 3 minutes
and serve

114

Other meat recipes

Rabbit
Rabbit stew
Ingredients:

    2 rabbits with the meat cut into bite size pieces
    4 slices of bacon
    1 tbsp of cooking oil
    1 cup of flour
    Salt and pepper to taste
    3 cups of chicken broth
    1 lb of mushrooms
    4 medium potatoes cut into small pieces
    3 medium onions
    3 crushed cloves of garlic
    ¼ cup of parsley
    Salt and pepper to taste
    ¼ tsp of cayenne
    1 cup of sour cream
    1 tbsp of parsley
    1 tbsp of paprika

Preparation:
Fry bacon in an oven proof skillet until brown and crisp and remove the bacon
Add in the oil to the bacon drippings
Place the flour, salt and pepper in a plastic bag
Place the rabbit pieces in the bag and shake it to coat it well
Fry the floured rabbit in the skillet until brown on all sides
Add the chicken broth, mushrooms, potatoes, onions, garlic, parsley, salt, pepper, cayenne and bacon pieces
Cover and bake it in oven at 350° F for 60 minutes
Remove from oven and stir in the sour cream
Garnish with parsley and paprika (or other seasonings to taste)
Serve with rice or bread

Rabbit stew
Ingredients:
- 1 Rabbit with the meat cut into bite size pieces
- 3 tbsp of butter
- 1 tsp of salt
- ½ tsp of ground black pepper
- 3 tbsp of flour
- ½ cup of beef or vegetable broth
- ½ cup of white wine
- 6 slices of bacon
- 6 medium onions
- 4 crushed cloves of garlic
- 1 lb of sliced mushrooms

Preparation:
Wash, and dry the rabbit pieces
Melt the butter in a baking pan
Brown the sides of the rabbit pieces
Sprinkle the rabbit pieces with the salt, pepper and flour
Continue to brown them
Add the broth, wine and bring to a boil
Cover and cook them over low heat for 60 minutes until tender
While the rabbit is cooking, brown the bacon in a skillet
Add the onions and sauté them until they are translucent
Add the garlic, mushrooms and sauté them for 4 minutes
Add this mixture to the rabbit and cook for 20 minutes until the rabbit is tender
If needed add more beef broth or wine while cooking
Serve

Rabbit pie
Making the Pie crust
Ingredients: 3 cups of flour
½ tsp of salt
1 cup of margarine
1/3 cup of cold water

Preparation:
Mix flour and salt in large bowl
Blend 2/3 of the cup of margarine into the flour
The mixture should have a texture like cornmeal
Add the rest of the margarine until it crumbs like the size of peas
Sprinkle 1 tbsp of water at a time, over the mixture tossing it with a fork
The particles should stick together
- Using too much water will make the pie crust dough sticky and the pastry tough
- Too little water will make the dough crumbly and hard to work with
Gently form a ball by pressing the particles together
Wrap the ball in plastic and refrigerate for 45 minutes
Then divide the ball of dough in half
(One for the bottom of the pie crust and the other for the top)
Then sprinkle a flat work surface lightly with flour
Flatten the ½ of dough gently and sprinkle the top with flour
Rub some flour onto a rolling pin.
Roll the dough from the centre to the edge in all directions
Form a circle about 2" wider than the pie pan
Turn the pie crust dough while rolling
This will stop it from sticking to your work surface
If needed dust it with more flour

Make a second one similarly for the top of the pie

Ingredients to fill the pie:
    4 cups of rabbit meat cut in bite-size pieces
    3 tbsp of cooking oil
    1 large chopped onion
    1 cup of diced carrots
    1 cup of diced potatoes
    ½ cup of peas
    3 cups of vegetable or beef broth

Preparation:
Heat the cooking oil in a large skillet
Add and sauté the onions and then remove them

Toss the rabbit pieces in a bag mixed with flour, salt, pepper and spices
Put the meat in the skillet with the remaining flour mixture and cook until browned
Add the broth and bring it to a boil
Cover the skillet and simmer for about 30 minutes
Add the potatoes, carrots, peas and simmer for 30 minutes
Then add the onions back to meat mixture

Finish the pie
   Fold the first flattened pie crust dough in half, then in half again to form a 1/4 circle
   Unfold and ease it into a pan that has been lightly buttered
   It should cover the bottom and the sides
   Prick some holes in it with a fork
   Bake it for about 5 minutes until slightly brown
   Fill the pie crust with the meat mixture
   Salt and pepper to taste
   Cover the ingredients with the second pie crust
   Wet the edge and press the top and bottom crusts together with a fork
   Make two small slits in the top of the crust
   Bake at 350° F for 30 minutes or until brown
   Serve

Rabbit roasting
To roast a rabbit, fold its front legs into its rib cavity and tie its back legs together
(You may stuff the rabbit with your favourite stuffing)
Baste the rabbit with butter
Sprinkle a little seasoning of your choice over it (Possibly thyme, salt and pepper)
Roast at 400° F for 30 minutes and then turn the heat down to 350 degrees
Continue cooking for another 30 minutes or until done

Wild boar
As a roasted leg
Refrigerate a leg of wild boar (about 5 lbs) for 12 hours

Ingredients:

For the marinade:
    2 carrots cut in ½ inch pieces
    2 medium sliced onions
    5 cups of red wine
    2 bay leaves
    5 crushed cloves
    1 tsp of thyme

To roast the wild boar:
    4 tbsp of cooking oil
    15 whole cloves

For the sauce:
    3 cups of chicken stock
    1 cup of raisons

Place the wine, herbs, spices and vegetables in a medium-sized saucepan
Bring it to a boil over medium high heat and cook for about 5 minutes
Remove from the heat and let it cool
Strain it and mix in the vinegar
Pour it over the wild boar and return it to the refrigerator for 12 hours
Turn it every 8 hours in the marinade

Remove
Salt and pepper to taste
Preheat the oven to 450°F
Remove the leg of wild boar from the marinade (keep the marinade)

Make tiny slits all over it and insert a garlic clove into each slit
Place the boar in a baking pan and pour some of the marinade over it
Roast it in the oven for up to 2 hours until golden brown
Keep marinating it every 25 minutes
When roasted remove it from the oven onto a platter
Let it rest for 25 minutes

Remove the juice and browned bits from the bottom of the baking pan
Place it in a saucepan and pour in the chicken stock
Bring it to a boil over medium-high heat
Reduce by half and then stir in the raisons
Cook until the sauce is smooth for about 15 minutes
Remove from the heat to a carving board
Slice the wild boar and arrange it on a platter
Pour the sauce over the meat and garnish to taste
Serve

As roasted rack of ribs
Refrigerate in a dish for 12 hours
Remove
Salt, pepper and season to taste
Preheat the oven to 450°F
Roast it in the oven for up to 2 hours until golden brown

As tenderloin
Lay the tenderloin to rest until it comes to room temperature
Rub it with cooking oil
Salt and pepper to taste

Pre-heat the oven to 400° F
Combine maple syrup with apple cider vinegar to taste
Use a non-aluminium pot
Bring to a boil for 6 minutes
Simmer at medium heat until it has reduced to syrup and place aside

In a separate large heated pan add 3 tbsp of oil
Brown the tenderloin to a crust on all sides
Then place it in a baking dish in a preheated oven for about 12 minutes
(Adjust the minutes according to the size of the tenderloin)
Remove it and let it rest for 12 minutes
Add 3 tbsp of apple cider vinegar to the pan and scrape off the pieces
Add this to the thickened syrup
Pour over the sliced tenderloin
Serve

Wild Boar curried stew
Ingredients:
- 1 lb of cubed boar meat
- 6 slices of bacon
- 1 chopped onion
- 2 crushed garlic cloves
- 2 tbsp of curry powder
- 1 cup of water
- 2 tbsp of parsley
- 1 cup of sliced tomatoes
- 1 cup of sliced carrots
- 2 medium cut potatoes
- 2 tbsp of cornstarch

Preparation:
Fry the bacon in a skillet until crisp
Remove the bacon, crumble it and set it aside
Pour off most of the bacon grease
Sear and cook the boar meat cubes in the remaining grease until meat is browned
Add the onion, garlic, 1 tbsp of curry powder and stir
Stir in 1 cup of water
Remove from heat and set aside
Combine the parsley, tomatoes, carrots and potatoes in a casserole dish

Add the meat mixture and mix in 1 tbsp on curry powder
Bake at 350° F for up to 60 minutes until the meat and veg-
etables are tender
Serve

Wild boar cleaned intestines
Used as casings for Italian sausage or Bratwurst

Bacon
> This cut of meat is taken from the sides, belly, or back of
> a hog or wild boar
> It may be cured, smoked, or both
> Chicken or turkey skin may also be used similarly as
> bacon
> Eggplant bacon – Sliced in long slices – seasoned and
> dehydrated until crisp

Wild boar quarters **(smoked)**
> Season the meat with salt, pepper and garlic
> Completely wrap the meat so the vapours and drippings
> are locked in
> Slowly smoke-bake it at about 300° F, rotating it to
> ensure even cooking
> The time will vary depending on the size of the Boar
> (usually about 6 hours)

Deer
Venison Stroganoff
Ingredients:
- 1 lb of cubed Venison pieces
- 2 diced Onions
- 4 cloves of crushed Garlic
- 2 cups of sliced mushrooms
- 3 tbsp of cooking Oil
- Salt and pepper to taste
- 1 cup of cream
- 1 cup of noodles

Preparation:
Heat cooking oil in a frying pan, add the venison and brown
Add the Cream and stir
Add salt and pepper to taste
Bring to a boil and turn to a low heat
Cover and simmer for at 45 minutes until tender
Separately boil the noodles until ready (6-10 minutes)
Strain the Noodles and place on a platter
Pour the venison over the noodles and serve

Deer stew
Ingredients:
- 1½ lb of cubed Venison pieces
- 2 diced Onions
- 3 cloves of crushed Garlic
- 3 tbsp of Oil
- 2 cups of sliced mushrooms
- 2 cups of sliced carrots
- 2 cups of cut potatoes
- 1 cup of sliced celery
- ½ cup of diced tomato
- 1 cup of wine
- 1 cup of raisons
- 1 cup of vegetable stock
- Salt and pepper to taste

Preparation:
Add the Oil to a large skillet and heat
Add the Venison and brown for about 3 minutes
Add the Garlic, Mushrooms and Onions and mix for 3 minutes
Add the vegetable stock
Add the sliced carrots
Add the potato pieces
Add the sliced celery
Add the diced tomato
Add the wine
Add the raisons
Add salt and pepper to taste
Bring to a boil
Turn the heat to low and simmer for 4 to 6 hours with the lid on until done
Serve with rice

Deer kebabs
Ingredients:
  (The following alternated pieces)
  Deer meat cut in 1 inch cubes
  Cherry tomatoes
  Small mushroom caps
  Small onions
  Pieces of green peppers
  Zucchini pieces

  Marinade:
  1 cup of oil
  1 cup of red wine
  ¼ cup of lemon juice
  3 crushed Garlic cloves
  2 tbsp Worcestershire sauce
  Salt and pepper to taste

Preparation:
Mix the marinade ingredients in a bowl and set the meat cubes in it for 3 hours
Alternate the marinated deer meat with the vegetables on skewers
Grill them, turning and basting them with remaining marinade for 12 minutes
Serve

Deer roast
Ingredients:
    A large cut of deer roast
    8 cloves of garlic
    2 sticks of sliced celery
    3 diced onions
    ½ cup of oil
    Salt and pepper
    2 cups of gravy

Preparation:
Make slits in the roast with a knife (about 1 inch wide and 2 inches deep)
Stuff the onion and garlic into the slits
Add the salt and pepper to taste
Place the meat in a refrigerator for 6 hours
Heat the oil in an iron skillet
Brown the meat on both sides
Add the onion, celery and garlic
Add water to cover half of the skillet
Bring the water to a boil and cover the skillet
Cook at medium temperature for about 3 hours
Add the carrots and potatoes and cook for 30 minutes
Add the gravy and cook for 10 minutes
Serve

Chickweed stew

1 pound of meat – browned in an iron pot with cooking oil or butter
Add 1 cup of wild onions and sauté
Pour in 1 cup of water
Simmer for 60 minutes
Add 3 cups of chickweed
Add a sliced large tomato or 10 autumn olive berries
Simmer for 25 minutes
Add seasoning to taste
(Possibly parsley, thyme, salt and pepper)
Simmer for 5 minutes
Serve

Cajun gumbo

Heat iron skillet with 3 tbsp of oil
Sauté and brown 2 cups of sausage meat in the skillet
Add I large diced onion and 3 crushed cloves of garlic
Mix in 2 cups of cooked chicken pieces and brown
Add some flour, oil and stir for 12 minutes, making rue
Sauté slices of 1 onion, 1 bell pepper, and 3 sticks of sliced celery in a skillet
Add it to the chicken, sausage and rue mixture
Add
1 cup of diced tomatoes
½ cup of green onion tops
1 cup of kidney beans
4½ cups of chicken or vegetable stock
½ tsp of red pepper
Salt & pepper to taste
1 bay leaf
Simmer for 35 minutes
Serve with crusty bread or rice

Chapter Seven: Wild plant and other categorized recipes

Flower petal lamb delicacy
Ingredients:
  1 lb of mixed flower petals
  (Honeysuckle, violet, rose, squash or other)
  2 tbsp of oil
  2 tbsp of butter
  2 lbs of lamb pieces
  2 onions
  2 cloves of crushed garlic
  1 sliced bell pepper
  Salt and black pepper to taste
  1 tbsp of lime juice
  1 tbsp of grated nutmeg
  2 cups of white wine

Preparation:
Wash the flower petals and place them in a bowl
Heat the oil and butter and brown the meat in a pot (remove the meat)
Reduce the heat, add and sauté the onion
Add the garlic, bell pepper, lime juice and nutmeg
Return the meat to the pot
Add the white wine and season
Simmer for 90 minutes, or until meat is tender
Move it several times to prevent it from sticking to the pot
Add more wine if necessary
Cook uncovered until the gravy is reduced
Gently add the flower petals and don't stir (Don't break up the petals)
Serve

Frog legs
Detach and fry them like chicken legs (Kentucky)
or
Sprinkle spices on the frog legs and sauté them in oil
(Use hot spices like cayenne pepper or flavour them with milder spices)
Sauté the frog legs until they are tender
or

Living in Difficult Times

Soak the frog legs in salt water for one hour
Heat vegetable oil in a skillet to 375° F
Roll the frog legs in flour and flavour them with spices
Fry them in a skillet until they are golden brown
or
Set the oven to broil
Line a shallow pan with aluminium foil and add the frog legs
Cover the frog legs with lemon juice and flavour them with spices
Wrap the foil around the legs to form a packet, and place the pan in the oven
Broil the frog legs until they are tender
Serve

Squirrel stew
Ingredients:
   4 cups of squirrel meat bite-size pieces
   1 cup of flour
   2 tbsp of oil
   4 strips of bacon
   1 cup of sliced carrots
   1 cup of diced onions
   1 cup of cut celery
   1 cup of Wine (good tasting)
   ½ cup of diced tomato
   2 cups of vegetable stock
   1 tsp each of thyme and sage to season
   Salt and pepper to taste

Preparation:
Sauté the onions, carrots, celery in oil, in a pot and set aside
Roll the squirrel pieces in flour
Add the bacon to a separate pan and fry until crisp
Add the squirrel and brown it in the pan for about 5 minutes
Add the wine and tomato to the pan and stir for 5 minutes
Now place the mixture on the vegetables in the pot
Add the vegetable stock
Add the salt, pepper, thyme and sage
Simmer for I hour
Serve

Turtle
Some of the meat of a Snapping turtle has the texture of frog legs or lobster
Its four legs and tail have a dark meat
The neck and back straps have white meat

Turtle stew
Ingredients:
> 2 lbs of rinsed Turtle meat cut into bite-size pieces (dark or white meat)
> 10 pieces of bacon
> 1 cup of flour
> 4 cups of broth (chicken or beef)
> 3 sliced carrots
> 4 large cubed potatoes
> 2 chopped onions
> 1 can of diced tomatoes
> 1 tbsp of thyme
> 2 tsp marjoram
> Salt and pepper to taste

Preparation:
Fry the bacon in a large pot until crisp and set aside
Season the turtle pieces with salt and pepper
Cover them with flour
Brown them in the bacon grease over medium heat
Add 4 cups beef broth and bring it to a boil
Reduce heat and simmer until turtle is tender
Remove the turtle and allow cooling
Remove the meat from the bones
Place them in the pot with the vegetables and simmer for 30 minutes
Add seasonings to taste
Serve

Fish

Watercress and fish

Place water 1½ inches deep in a pot and bring to a boil

Place the fish in a steamer basket above the boiling water with the skin-side down

Salt and pepper to taste

Completely cover the fish with the watercress and season to taste

(Be careful not to burn your fingers)

Cover the pot

Cook until the steamed watercress is wilted and the fish is translucent in the centre

(About 7 minutes for a 2 inch thick fish fillet)

Melt butter in a saucepan (2 tbsp of butter per fish)

Mix in ½ cup of sorrel leaves or 2 tbsp of lemon juice (per fish)

Pour the mixture over the fish and serve

Watercress fish cakes

Ingredients:

2 lbs of potatoes

2 lbs of steamed fish

(Steamed in a basket over boiling water with the skin-side down)

Remove the skin and flake the fish from the bones

3 oz of butter

6 handfuls of finely chopped watercress (Washed clean)

2 eggs

Plate of breadcrumbs or flour

2 tbsp of cooking oil

Flour

Preparation:

Boil the potatoes for up to 30 minutes and mash

Stir in the flaked fish

Add the melted butter and watercress

Mix and form into round balls 3 inches in diameter

Flatten the balls on a floured surface

Remove and place in a refrigerator for 30 minutes
Then submerge each cake into a beaten egg wash
Gently cover each cake with breadcrumbs or flour
Fry each side carefully in hot oil for 4 minutes until brown and serve

Crab cakes
Ingredients:
    4 cups of minced crab meat
    3 cups of seasoned bread crumbs
    3 lightly beaten eggs
    1 cup of green onions
    1 cup of mayonnaise
    2 tbsp of butter
    2 tbsp of lemon juice
    4 crushed cloves of Garlic
    ½ tsp of red pepper
    Salt and pepper to taste

Preparation:
Combine the ingredients
Divide into small balls (golf ball size)
Flatten the balls to cakes ½ inch thick
Cover with bread crumbs
Heat oil in a skillet
Gently fry each side until golden brown
Remove so as not to break
Serve

Trout, bass, walleyes and crappie
Cover the fillet fish in flour
Dip the fish in a beaten egg wash
Cover with the flour, meal, nuts or seed
Shallow fry them at medium heat for about 5 minutes on both sides
Serve

Fish stuffing
Ingredients:
Mix bread crumbs, ground nuts and water cress leaves
Then mix with Cream or Mayonnaise (possibly a little mustard)
Stuff in the cleaned cavity of the fish and then grill or fry

Rainbow trout or brown trout
Ingredients:
   4 fish gutted, scaled and cleaned
   2 cups of finely chopped nuts
   1 cup of sliced prunes or raisons
   ½ cup of sweet wine
   3 cups of fresh breadcrumbs
   Salt and pepper to taste
   1 lemon
   1 tsp of chopped parsley
   1 tsp of chopped dill
   ¼ cup of chopped chives
   2 tbsp of cooking oil

Preparation:
Mix the nuts, breadcrumbs, prunes/raisons and wine
Mix in the salt, pepper, parsley and dill
Place the mixture into the cavity of the fish
Close and secure it (possibly with toothpicks)
Heat oil in a pan and fry the fish for 5 minutes on each side
Squeeze the lemon juice over it
Garnish it with the chopped chives
Serve

Smallmouth bass or rock bass - crumbed
Ingredients:
   4 fillet fish
   4 cups of bread crumbs
   3 tbsp of vegetable oil
   1 tbsp of butter
   4 small onions finely sliced
   4 tsp of oregano
   4 cloves of garlic

Salt and pepper to taste
½ cup of parmesan cheese
½ cup of grated cheddar cheese
4 tbsp of lemon juice

Preparation:
Pre-heat the oven to 350° F
Heat 3 tbsp of cooking oil and 1 tbsp of butter in an oven proof dish
Sprinkle both sides of the bass with lemon juice
Season with salt, pepper, oregano and lay in the dish
Mix the bread crumbs, oil, onion, garlic and cheese
Place the mixture over the fish
Bake in the oven for 15 minutes until golden brown
Serve

Rainbow trout or Crappie
Heat a pan with 3 tbsp of cooking oil and add 1 tbsp of butter
Sprinkle parsley and oregano over the oil and butter
Dredge each fillet fish in an egg wash
Cover both sides with flour
Dredge each fillet fish again in the egg wash
Cover both sides with crumbs
Salt & pepper to taste
Carefully fry each fish on each side until brown for about 5 minutes
Serve with vegetables and a garnished baked potato

Walleyes
Ingredients:
    5 fillet walleyes
    1 bay leaf
    1 cup of flour
    1 tbsp of thyme
    1 diced onion
    ½ cup of crushed tomato
    8 tbsp of vegetable oil
    4 cloves of minced garlic

3 tbsp of chopped parsley
2 cups of red wine
1 cup of boiling water
Salt and pepper to taste

Preparation:
Salt and pepper the fillet fish
Dredge both sides in the flour
Shake off excess flour
Sauté the onion in 3 tbsp of oil in an iron skillet until translucent
Add the garlic for about 2 minutes
Stir in 2 tablespoons flour for about two minutes
Turn off the heat
Add the wine, boiling water and stir
Turn on the heat until the sauce thickens
Add the bay leaf, thyme, tomato and simmer
Heat the remaining oil in a large pan
Sear the fish on each side
Pour the sauce over the fish and simmer for about 20 minutes
Season with salt, pepper
Garnish with the chopped parsley
Serve

Catfish
Ingredients:
4 lb of fillet catfish
½ cup of cornmeal
½ cup of flour
2 beaten eggs
½ cup of finely minced onion
3 cups of oil
Salt and pepper to taste

Preparation:
Mix the flour, cornmeal, salt, and pepper in a bowl
In a separate bowl beat the eggs and mix in the minced onions

Heat the vegetable oil in a pan
Dredge both sides of the catfish in the egg mixture and cover with flour
Carefully fry both sides for about 6 minutes until golden brown
Serve

Cleaning off fish scales and the fish
Place the fish on a board
Use a spoon to scrape off the scales against the lay of the scales
Do this on both sides of the fish
Remove the fish from the board, discard the scales
Remove the tail, head, gut and clean the fish

Some of the sites I have watched:
How to clean and pan cook fish -
http://www.youtube.com/watch?v=u3iDdPfUX5g&NR=1&feature=fvwp
Gutting fish
http://www.youtube.com/watch?v=AZh6IMPvR_o&feature=related
How to filet Walleyes
http://www.youtube.com/watch?v=h2njws7UYFg

Other favorites

Stinging nettle fritters
(Wear gloves when handling stinging nettle)
Ingredients:
> 6 cups of young stinging nettle leaves
> 3 large cloves of garlic
> 5 tbsp of bread crumbs
> Salt and pepper to taste
> ¼ tsp of baking soda
> 2 eggs

Preparation:
Allow the stinging nettle leaves to soak in water overnight
Then cook for 6 minutes in boiling water
(This process will neutralize any toxicity in the plant)
Mince the cooked leaves
Add the crumbs, eggs, garlic, baking soda and seasoning
Mix well and leave for 50 minutes
Shape to the size of small golf balls and flatten into fritters
Fry them in oil for 3 minutes on each side
Serve

Bean pottage
Ingredients:
> Cook 2 cups of pinto beans for 1 hour
> Sauté 2 onions in 2 tbsp of oil in a skillet and add to the beans
> Add 2 slices of ham or bacon
> Add salt and pepper to taste

Preparation:
Cook for 60 minutes
Add 2 lbs of greens of your choice and simmer for 45 minutes
Salt and pepper to taste
Serve

Autumn olive sauce
> Simmer autumn olive berries over low heat until soft (as many as required)

Strain out the seeds (If so desired)
Salt and pepper and season to taste
Use as a sauce on pancakes or other dishes

Quiche – lamb quarter greens
Ingredients:
  2 sliced onions
  1 tbsp of cooking oil
  4 cups of lamb quarter greens
  3 cups of milk
  6 eggs
  2 cups of cheese
  1 pie shell (or make one – see chicken pie crust recipe)
  Salt, pepper and seasonings to taste

Preparation:
Sauté the onions in the oil in a pot until tender
Add 4 cups of chopped lamb quarter greens
Cover and remove from heat
Mix in a separate bowl, 3 cups of milk, 6 eggs and 1 cup of cheese
Mix it in with the lamb's quarters
Salt, pepper and season to taste
Pour into the pie shell
Sprinkle with 1 cup cheese
Bake at 350° F for 45 minutes or until a golden brown
Allow it to stand for 12 minutes and serve

Frittata
Ingredients:
  16 oz of spinach (or lambs quarters and other greens)
  2 large diced onions
  1 diced Red bell pepper
  1 cup of cooked diced potatoes (or potato substitute)
  6 beaten eggs
  ½ cup of mozzarella cheese
  ¼ cup of parmesan cheese
  2 tbsp of cooking oil
  Salt and pepper to taste

Preparation:
Add the spinach/greens to a pan and cook to wilt
Remove for later use
Sauté the onions with oil in pan
Add in the red bell pepper
Add the cooked potatoes
Add the spinach
Separately whisk the eggs and add the salt and pepper to taste
Pour gently into the pan and mix with the other ingredients
Cook for about 8 minutes
Sprinkle the parmesan cheese on top
Broil for about 5 minutes
Serve

Pasta
Cattail pasta
　Ingredients:
　20 oz of pasta
　4 tbsp of oil
　2 cups of peeled, sliced, cleaned cattail shoots or cucumbers
　4 sliced cloves of garlic
　½ cup of parsley
　Salt and pepper to taste

Preparation:
Cook the pasta in salted water along with 1 tbsp of oil until al dente and drain in a colander
Heat 3 tbsp of oil in a skillet
Add and sauté the cattail shoots over medium heat for 12 minutes
Add the garlic and sauté for another 3 minutes
Add the pasta
Salt and pepper to taste
Heat and sprinkle the parsley over the top and serve

Poke Casserole
Ingredients:
  7 cups of chopped young poke leaves
  (Forage from under 10 inch high plants, only in springtime)
  2 Eggs
  1 lb of ground meat
  5 tbsp of oil
  ½ cup of bread crumbs
  5 cloves of chopped garlic
  1 tsp of ground tarragon
  Seasoning:
  ¼ tsp turmeric
  ¼ tsp paprika
  1 tsp of mustard
  Salt and pepper to taste

Preparation:
Rapidly boil the poke leaves in a large pot of water
Drain in a colander
Add fresh water and boil again for another 2 minutes
Drain and add fresh water and boil again for 20 minutes
Drain again in a colander and press out all the water
Then mix in the meat and eggs
Mix in 3 tbsp of oil, 5 cloves of chopped garlic, ¼ cup of vinegar, 2 tsp soy sauce
Then add and mix in the cooked poke
Add salt, pepper and seasonings to taste
Add that to an oiled casserole dish
Mix 2 tbsp of oil with the bread crumbs
Cover the poke mixture with it
Bake uncovered for 30 minutes in a preheated 375° F oven until slightly brown
Serve

Alfredo penne pasta

Boil 1 lb of penne pasta in salted water for about 6 minutes until al dente
Drain out the water
Place in an oven proof casserole dish
Add 4 cups of small cooked and browned pieces of chicken
(Add fried shrimp if so desired)
Mix in Alfredo sauce
Salt and pepper to taste
Sprinkle on grated parmesan cheese
Lightly sprinkle rosemary and parsley on top
Bake in the oven for 5 minutes
Serve

Alfredo sauce recipe
Melt 1½ cups of butter
Add 4 cups of whipped cream
Add 2 cups of grated parmesan cheese
Simmer over very low heat stirring often for about 6 minutes
Use

Croquettes

Ingredients:
2 lbs of chopped meat cooked until tender
Seasoned with salt and pepper to taste
(Set aside about 2 cups of the seasoned cooked meat used for filling later)
½ pound of seasoned stuffing
1 cup of breadcrumbs
4 tbsp of oil
2 tbsp of flour
1 cup of milk

Preparation:
Heat oil in pan and stir in the flour
Gradually stir in the milk until it boils
Add the other cooked meat and seasoned stuffing
Divide it into 8 parts, each 4 inches in diameter
Flatten each piece to a ¼ inch thick
Flour them and let them cool

Place a small amount of meat as a filling in the middle of each flattened piece
Roll the flat pieces into neat tube like croquettes sealing in the meat
Drench each croquette with egg and then cover with breadcrumbs
Submerge and fry them in hot oil until golden brown
Remove and drain on a paper towel
Serve

Dumplings – with fillings
Ingredients:
  4 cups of flour
  1 tbsp of baking powder
  2 cups of milk
  Salt and pepper to taste
  4 cups of sliced greens fried with bacon (or other filling of your choice)

Preparation:
Mix the flour, milk, baking powder, salt, pepper and form 3 inch size balls
Flatten each ball to ¼ inch thick and place filling (greens) in the middle
Fold them over in a half circle and pinch them closed
Cook them in soup or stew for 10 minutes
Serve

Turnovers
Preparation:
12 Pastry squares – 6 inches wide
6 cups of cooked chopped greens mixed with 1 cup of cheese
Salt, pepper and seasonings to taste

Add a spoonful of the mixture on each pastry square
Fold the pastry square from corner to corner to form a triangle
Gently pinch the sides closed
Place the triangles on a baking sheet
Bake at 350° F in an oven for 20 minutes or until brown

Making the pastry for the turnovers:
    2 cups of flour
    ¼ teaspoon of salt
    3 sticks of butter
    6 tablespoons of ice water
Preparation:
Place the flour in a large bowl and add the salt
Cut the butter into small pieces and add to the flour
Mix the butter and flour thoroughly
Add ice water and stir gently with a fork
Knead the flour and butter mixture into the dough
Form it into a ball and place in the refrigerator for 30 minutes

Remove the dough ball from the refrigerator
Sprinkle a flat surface with flour
Place the dough ball on the surface and flatten it into a rectangular shape
Fold a third of one side to the centre
Then fold the other side over it
Roll it out and repeat this process one more time
Refrigerate for 30 minutes.
Sprinkle a flat surface with flour
Take the dough out of the refrigerator and place it on the flat surface
Roll it to a thickness of about 1/8 inch
Cut into 6 inch squares for the turnovers

Soufflé croissants
Ingredients:
- 3 tsp of butter
- 2 tbsp of flour
- 1cup of milk
- 2 egg yolks
- 4 egg whites
- 2 cooked sausage links cut in ½ inch slices
- 2 cups of cooked spinach
- 2 diced tomatoes
- 1 cup of grated cheese
- Salt, pepper and paprika to taste

Preparation:
Preheat oven to 350° F
Butter the inside of a soufflé dish
Melt the butter in a small pot and stir in the flour
Cook over low heat for 2 minutes and then remove from heat
Add the milk and whisk it
Add the salt, pepper and paprika
Simmer and stir at medium heat until it thickens
Remove from the heat and whisk in the egg yokes

Beat the egg white in a separate bowl until it puffs
Add ½ of it to a pot and mix in the sausage, spinach and tomato
Gently fold in the other ½ of egg white and cheese
Transfer it to the buttered soufflé dish
Place the dish on a baking sheet in the oven
Bake at 375° F for 20 minutes, until the top has browned

Use 4 croissants:
Cut open each croissant starting from the two points, backward
Do not completely cut through
Fold the croissants open like a book
Microwave for 10 seconds to soften
Place a scoop of the soufflé on each croissant
Fold the four corners of the croissant inward to close
Serve

Creamed watercress

Ingredients:
- 7 cups of watercress
- 3 tbsp butter or margarine
- 10 oz of chopped onions
- 3 cloves of minced garlic
- 3 tbsp of flour
- 1 cup of cream
- ½ tsp of nutmeg
- Salt and pepper to taste

Preparation:
Heat the butter or margarine in a pan
Sauté the onions and garlic until soft
Add flour and stir for about 3 minutes
Stir in the cream and nutmeg
Bring to a simmer and cook for 3 minutes
Add the watercress to the pan a little at a time
Stir until the watercress has wilted
Salt and pepper to taste
Serve

Mushroom / onion / green bean casserole

Sauté 1 cup of mushrooms and 1 sliced onion in an oiled skillet
Add and mix in some flour until the mixture is dry
Add 3 cups of green beans
Add 2 cups of chicken stock
Add 1 cup of cream
Boil for 6 minutes
Cover with French dried onions
Bake in oven until it browns for about 15 minutes
Serve

Pizza
Crust
Ingredients:
¼ oz envelope of Active Dry Yeast (about 2¼ tsp)
2 Cups of warm water
4 Cups of bread flour
1½ tsp of salt
2 tbsp of oil
1 tbsp of sugar

Preparation:
Pour the warm water in a large mixing bowl
Add the sugar and stir until dissolved
Add the yeast and gently stir the mixture until the yeast is dissolved
Let sit for 12 minutes for the yeast to foam
Stir in the salt and oil
Whisk in 1 cup of flour until it is dissolved
Add the second cup of flour and whisk it in until smooth
Evenly mix in the 3rd cup of flour and it will thicken
Mix in the 4th cup of flour
(If needed add flour to reduce the stickiness of the dough)
Fold the dough mixture into itself, over and over again
It will absorb all of the moisture and firm into a mass
Now knead it on a floured flat surface
Press the dough outwards with both your hands
Fold the mass in half and push it into itself, again and again for up to 20 minutes
The dough ball will become pliable and elastic
Coat the dough ball with a thin layer of oil
Coat a large mixing bowl on the inside with oil
Place the ball of dough at the bottom of the mixing bowl
Cover the top of the bowl and place it in a warm place about 85° F
Allow the dough to rise for up to 80 minutes
The dough will grow to at least twice its original size
Take it out of the bowl and cut it in half with a knife
Separately flatten each on a flat surface

Press out the air and form each portion into a smooth ball
From underneath, fold and tuck each portion into itself
Roll out each dough ball into a 3/8 inch thick flat circle,
about 14 inches in diameter
Place into a pizza pan
Allow it to rest for 12 minutes before adding the sauce,
cheese and toppings on top

Bake:
Place an oven rack in the middle of the oven
Heat the oven to 450° F and place the pizza with its toppings
on a flat pan
Let it bake for about 15 minutes or until done
Remove from oven, cut and serve

Pizza Toppings (prepared for a 14 inch diameter pizza)

Pepperoni topping
   Pour about 10 oz of tomato paste into the middle of the
   14 inch dough
   Spread the sauce evenly over the surface
   Leave an un-sauced 1 inch of the dough around the
   border
   (This will create a puffed up edge around the pizza)
   Sprinkle about 2 cups of shredded cheese evenly over
   the sauce
   Choose and place any combination of toppings you want
   on the pizza
   Finish off the top of the pizza with a cup of cheese
   Bake for 6 minutes
   Remove from oven, cut and serve

Cheese, Sausage and Pepperoni topping
10 oz of tomato paste
3 cups of different cheeses
Sausage and pepperoni

Chapter Seven: Wild plant and other categorized recipes

Vegetable topping
10 oz of tomato paste
3 cups of cheese
3 cups of cut vegetables

Fruit topping
    3 cups of fruit paste (Use instead of tomato paste)
    3 cups of cut fruit

Breakfast pizza
Ingredients:
    16 oz of pork sausage
    1 chopped onion
    2 tbsp of cooking oil
    ½ chopped green bell pepper
    ½ chopped red bell pepper
    16 oz of cream cheese
    1 diced tomato
    1 cup of scrambled egg
    1 cup of grated cheese
    Salt and pepper to taste

Preparation:
Cook sausage and onion in an oiled skillet until brown
Stir in the cream cheese until melted
Add and stir in the bell peppers, egg and tomato
Take a pizza crust – see above how to make a pizza crust
Spread the ingredients on top
Sprinkle grated cheese over it
Bake for about 6 minutes
Remove from oven, cut and serve

Cornmeal biscuits

Ingredients
- 4 cups of self-rising flour
- 1 cup of cornmeal
- 1 cup of butter cut in pieces
- 2 cups of buttermilk
- ½ cup of milk

Preparation:
Mix the flour and cornmeal in a bowl
Mix in the butter until crumbly
Stir in the buttermilk until the ingredients are moist
Place the dough on a floured surface and knead 3 times
Flatten the dough to a ½ inch thickness
Cut into 3 inch diameter round pieces
Place on a lightly greased baking sheet
Brush the tops with milk
Bake at 425° F for 13 minutes or until golden brown
Serve

Pies
Pot pie
Chicken / Turkey Pot Pie
Ingredients:
- 4 cups of diced chicken or turkey meat, washed and drained
- 3 tbsp of cooking oil
- 2 cups of water
- 1½ cups of mixed vegetables
- 2 finely sliced celery stalks
- 1 medium chopped onion
- 4 tbsp of minced fresh parsley
- I tbsp of baking soda
- Salt and pepper to taste

Preparation:
Preheat oven to 350° F
Lightly brown the meat in a skillet with the cooking oil
Add the water, mixed vegetables, celery, onions and parsley
Cook for 15 minutes
Mix baking soda in a ½ cup of water and add to the mixture
Stir the mixture adding salt and pepper to taste
Cook until it thickens for about 5 minutes
Then pour into a 9 inch pie crust (see pie crust recipe below)
Cover it with the second pie crust, wet the edge and press it down with a fork
Make 2 slits in the top of the crust and bake at 350° F for 30 minutes until brown
Serve

Pepper Steak or Rabbit Pie
Ingredients:
  4 cups of steak or rabbit meat cut in bite-size cubes or pieces
  3 tbsp of cooking oil
  1 chopped onion
  1 cup of diced carrots
  1 cup of diced potatoes
  3 cups of vegetable or beef broth
  Salt and pepper to taste

Preparation:
Heat the cooking oil in a large skillet
Sauté the onions until soft and set aside
Combine and mix the flour, salt, pepper and rabbit pieces in a bowl
Place the meat in a skillet and brown
Add the broth and bring to a boil
Cover skillet and simmer for about 50 minutes, or until meat is tender
Add potatoes and carrots and simmer for about 20 minutes
Add onions that were set aside

Living in Difficult Times

Place the first piecrust at the bottom of the pie pan to cover the bottom and side
Fill the pie crust with the ingredients
Cover with the second pie crust, wet the edge and press it down with a fork
Make two slits in the top of the crust, bake at 350° F for 30 minutes until brown and serve

Pie crust
Ingredients:
   2½ cups of all purpose flour
   ½ tsp of salt
   1 cup of margarine
   1/3 cup of cold water

Preparation:
Mix flour and salt in large bowl
Mix in about 2/3 of a cup of cut pieces of the margarine into the flour
The mixture should have a texture like cornmeal
Then mix in the rest of the shortening until it crumbs like the size of peas
Sprinkle 1 tablespoon of water at a time over the mixture
Toss it with a fork until the particles stick together and gently form a ball
Adding too much water will make the dough sticky and the pastry tough
Not adding enough water will make the dough crumbly and hard to work with
Wrap it in plastic and refrigerate for 30 minutes
Divide the ball of dough in half
(One for the bottom pie crust and the other for the top)
Sprinkle a flat surface with flour
Gently flatten ½ inch thickness of dough and sprinkle the top with flour
Rub some flour over a rolling pin
Roll from the centre to edge of the dough, in all directions about 1/8 inch thick

Make the circle of the first piece about 2" wider than the pie pan
It won't stick to the working surface if you sprinkle it with flour
Place it at the bottom of the pie pan
Make a second one similarly for the top of the pie crust

Soft and hard tacos

Soft taco
Fill the tortilla/fajita with the following -
Use any combination of the following ingredients:
Pieces of meat, chopped greens, tomato, grated cheese, sour cream and taco sauce
You may use beef or chicken
Salt and pepper to taste
Fold the sides of the tortilla/fajita inwards and then roll it to enclose the filling
Serve

Breakfast soft taco
Fill the tortilla/fajita with the following -
Use any combination of the following ingredients:
Scrambled egg, small cooked potato pieces, sausage and grated cheese
Salt and pepper to taste
Hot sauce – optional
Fold the sides of the tortilla/fajita inwards and then roll it to enclose the filling
Serve

Tortilla or fajita
Ingredients
    20 oz of plain flour
    ½ tsp of baking powder
    Salt to taste
    8 oz of butter (or margarine)
    ½ cup of warm water

Preparation:
Pour the flour, baking powder, salt into a large bowl and cut in the butter
Slowly pour in the water and mix until it becomes pliable dough
Knead the dough on a flat surface for about 15 minutes until smooth and elastic
Divide into 10 pieces and roll each piece to form a flat circle about a 1/8 inch thick
Cover to prevent them drying out
Heat an iron skillet or pan
Place each tortilla in the skillet for 1-2 minutes on each side, until a golden colour
Keep them warm in a covered dish until all have been cooked
Serve

Hard taco shell
Fold a tortilla/fajita in half with the two sides facing upwards (in a holder)
Bake or microwave it that way to harden
Fill it with the following ingredients:
Sausage meat, then sour cream, greens, tomato, grated cheese and taco sauce
Serve

Fried squirrel cakes
Ingredients:
 Meat of 3 Squirrels
 1 diced onion
 1 cup of diced tomato
 1 cup of mashed potato
 1 cup of breadcrumbs
 Salt, pepper and seasoning to taste
 ½ cup of bacon drippings

Preparation:
Boil the squirrel meat in water for 30 minutes
Remove the meat from bones and grind coarsely
Add the onion, tomato, mashed potato, breadcrumbs and seasoning
Shape into 4 inch diameter balls
Flatten to ½ inch thick
Fry on both sides in a heated skillet in bacon drippings until golden brown
Serve

Chicken Liver Pate
Ingredients:
 1lb of cleaned and chopped chicken livers
 1 cup of butter
 2 chopped onions
 4 chopped cloves of garlic
 2 bay leaves
 1 cup of red wine (more or less according to the constituency you want)

Preparation:
Place the ingredients in a closed pot
Simmer for 70 minutes over low heat
Remove the bay leaves and blend in a blender
Place in a refrigerator for 3 hours
Serve on toast or a warm bagel

Mock Tuna Pate

Chop, rinse and soak 4 cups of walnuts in water for 1 hour

Blend them in a blender

Blend in the following -

(3 carrots, 3 celery sticks, 2 onions, 3 cloves of garlic and 1 cup of bread crumbs)

Add 4 tbsp of cooking oil (more or less according to the constituency you want)

Add 1 tsp of cumin and 1 tbsp of cilantro

Add salt, pepper to taste and blend Serve on toast or a warm bagel

Sushi

Add 1 cup of rice in 3 cups of water and add 1 tbsp of butter and ½ tsp of salt

Cook for about 30 minutes until the rice is soft and if needed add more hot water

Then keep the lid closed and set aside for 30 minutes to absorb the water

Place the amount needed on a mat on a table so that the mat is easy to roll

Spread and flatten a condensed sheet of rice over the top of the mat about ¼ thick

(The sheet of flattened rice should be 6 inches by 12 inches)

Place a seaweed sheet or a large edible green leaf on top of the flattened rice

Cut strips of raw cucumber, squash, peppers, avocado, tuna or salmon (of your choice)

- About ¼ inch thick, ½ inch wide and 3 inches long
- The avocado, salmon and tuna can be ¾ inch wide

Place them horizontally on the middle 3 inches of the rice, next to each other

Salt and pepper to taste

Carefully roll in the 6 inch part of the mat and sheet of rice
Roll it tightly, folding in the ingredients as you roll
The rice should completely enclose the ingredients
A thin layer of rice should be on the outside and the ingredients in the inside
Remove the mat and you should have a rolled sushi 12 inches long
Carefully place in a refrigerator for 30 minutes
Carefully cut the rolled sushi with a sharp knife into 1 inch slices (about 12 slices)
As an extra feature you may drizzle a sauce of your choice over the sushi
    - Honey mustard
    - Shrimp sauce (mayonnaise mixed with ketchup to taste)
    Serve

Oriental stir fry

Ingredients:
    1 cup of dandelion flowers
    1 cup of new daylily shoots – cut to bite size pieces
    1 cup of broken walnuts
    1 cup of bamboo centre slices
    1 cup mushrooms
    1 fruit cut into bite size pieces
    2 cups of meat cut into bite size pieces
    ½ cup of cooking oil

Preparation:
Place oil in a skillet or wok and heat
Brown the meat in the oil
Add the ingredients and sauté for 8 to10 minutes
Mix in a sauce (oriental or other) and then serve

Breads

Types:
- Cornbread
- Whole wheat bread
- Regular flour breads (using different kinds of flour)
- Pawpaw bread (Which has a rose colour)
- Banana bread
- Raison bread
- Date bread – or Honey Locust pods that are ground
(It may be used as a substitute for flour and dates)

Flour – ground or milled
Wheat or other substitutes for regular flour
Corn for cornmeal

Other sources ground into flour
Seeds:
Dock brown seeds
Crabgrass seeds
Amaranth seeds
Sheep sorrel seeds
Yellow dock seeds
Pumpkin seeds
Common lawn grass and marsh grass seeds make excellent flour
Short grass or long grass seeds-
Cut the top of the grass with the seed and place in a pillow case
Shake off the seeds dry them and grind to flour

Different nuts:
Walnut
Pecan
Hickory
Acorn (washed and prepared)
Beechnut
Chinquapins (Like small chestnuts)

Honey locust pods
Green brier (Smilax) roots
Cattail pollen (For very fine flour)
Cattail – rhizome centres (used during the harsh winter months)
Wild rice

Crabgrass flour

Place the crabgrass seeds in a grain mill and grind coarsely
Winnow it by pouring it from one bowl to another, 5 times
Wind will blow away the lighter plant material
Line a cookie sheet with parchment paper and pour a one-inch layer of the winnowed grain onto the sheet
Roast it at 400° F in an oven for about 50 minutes
Remove and allow to cool (not in a refrigerator)
Wash to strain out excessive charred dust
Let the grains dry again
With a grain mill grind it fine into flour
Sift the flour through a sieve into a bowl
Use

Acorn flour

Information:
Use acorns from White Oak and not Red Oak trees
Acorn meal may be substituted for one-fourth of the flour needed in a regular flour recipe
It has a slight sweetish taste
Preparation:
Collect the acorns
Remove the caps of the acorns
Crack the outer shell of the acorn with a nut cracker or pliers
Peel off the shell and use the inner nut kernel
Discard any soft, defective, mouldy acorns, or ones with tiny holes in them
Drying may be gradually done in the house at normal room temperature
Lay them one layer thick in a tray
Green acorns will take about 5 weeks to dry

Oven Drying:

Lay them one layer thick in a flat pan and warm in an oven at
175º F for 30 minutes
Leave the oven door slightly open to let the moisture escape
Oven drying is quick, will kill insect larva and eliminate mould
problems
However with this process, it may lose moisture and flavour
It only has a three months shelf life
Preparation:
Remove the cap of the acorns
Crack the outer shell of the acorn with a nut cracker or pliers
Peel off the shell and use the inner nut kernel

Whole Nutmeat Kernels
If they are sweet and not bitter, proceed to process them
If they are bitter then grind, boil and rinse them
This will allow the tannic acid to be removed
Crush or grind them with a hand grinder, a mill or flat rock
When blending, add water to create a liquid mush

Boiling method – (for whole nut or ground nuts)
Fill two pots with water
- First boil:
Boil the first pot of water
Add salt and then add the nuts
After 35 minutes the water will be brown
Strain out the acorns in a colander
- Second Boil:
Boil the second pot of clean water
Add salt and then add the nuts
After 35 minutes the water will be brown
Strain out the acorns
- Third Boil:
Repeat the process of the second boil instructions
Taste an acorn
The original bitterness should be gone and it should have a
sweet, nutlike flavour
If not, then boil a fourth time
Do not let the wet nuts sit for hours between boiling
Dry the nutmeats by regular drying or in an oven

Yeast and starters –
Yeast
Oregon grape – the leaves & fruit are covered with a substance used as yeast
Or
Yeast recipe -
Ingredients:
    4 cups of bran
    2 litres of water (not too hot)
    ¼ cup of hops
    ¼ cup of sugar
Directions:
Add the boiled water to the bran and strain it
Add in the hops and sugar
When it is bubbly and growing in the bowl, it is ready
Store in the refrigerator and use within 1 week

Potato yeast starter
Ingredients:
    2 large potatoes, peeled and boiled until soft
    2 tablespoons of flour
    2 cups of water (from the potatoes that were cooked)
    ½ tsp of active dry yeast
    ½ cup of unbleached flour
Directions:
Boil the potatoes
Keep separately 2 cups of the water in which the potatoes were boiled
When lukewarm add the dry yeast and mash it until smooth
Add 2 tablespoons of flour and stir until smooth
Stir in the 2 kept cups of the potato water and mix well
Stir in about ½ cup of flour, making a thin batter
Cover lightly with a damp cloth and keep in a warm place to rise
When it is light and bubbly, it is ready to be used
It may be kept like this in a covered jar for several days
Store in the refrigerator and use within 1 week

If the mixture is not used within a week, stir in another ½ cup of flour to feed it

The starter mixture should always smell like fresh yeast
Should any liquid accumulate, stir it down again
If it begins to acquire a sour odour, discard it
If starting over again from scratch, use utensils and containers that are cleaned well

Amish bread starter
Ingredients:
> One ¼ ounce package of active dry yeast
> ¼ cup of warm water (110° F)
> 3 cups of all-purpose flour
> 3 cups of white sugar
> 3 cups of milk

Directions:
In a small bowl, dissolve the yeast in water
Let it stand for 10 minutes
Combine 1 cup of flour and 1 cup of sugar in a large container
Slowly stir in 1 cup milk and mix well
Then dissolve the yeast with the warm water and add to the mixture
Cover loosely and let stand until it becomes bubbly
Leave it loosely covered at room temperature
(This is day 1 of a 10 day cycle)
Days 2 thru 4 - stir each day with a spoon
Day 5 - stir in 1 cup of flour, 1 cup of sugar and 1 cup of milk
Days 6 thru 9 - stir
Day 10 - Now use 1 cup to make your first bread
Then stir in 1 cup of flour, 1 cup of sugar and 1 cup of milk
Store 1 cup as a starter in the refrigerator
The remaining starter may be given away or discarded

Use that starter to begin the 10 day process over again (beginning with step 2)
Continue using a starter that way indefinitely
Once you have the starter, always ignore step 1
You may also freeze a starter in a 1 cup measure for later use
Frozen starters will take at least 3 hours at room temperature to thaw before using

Bread recipe
Ingredients:
  6 cups of bread flour
  ½ cup of sugar
  1 tablespoon of salt
  4 teaspoons of instant yeast
  1 cup of lukewarm water
  1 cup of buttermilk (not cold)
  ¼ cup of oil
  2 large beaten eggs

  Egg wash:
  1 egg white
  3 tablespoons of milk

Preparation:
Mix the water, buttermilk and oil
Then add 1½ cups of flour and mix until smooth
Stir in sugar, eggs and salt until smooth
Stir in the yeast
Let sit uncovered for 15 minutes
Gradually add in the flour until it becomes difficult to mix and sticky
Knead it for about 10 minutes until smooth and elastic
Place the dough into a lightly oiled bowl and cover with plastic wrap
Set aside in a warm place for about 60 minutes
Place on a lightly floured flat surface, cutting it in half
Roll and slightly press the dough, pinching the seam closed
Place each piece into a separate bread pan and plastic wrap for about 60 minutes
Remove the wrap and brush the top of the loaves with egg wash
Bake at 375° F for about 35 minutes
Remove the baked bread from pans, cool and enjoy

Rusk's – buttermilk (like biscotti)
Ingredients:
- 3 lbs of self-rising flour (proportionately substitute and add bran for roughage)
- ½ tbsp of salt
- ¾ lb of margarine
- 3 eggs
- 2 cups of sugar
- 2 cups of buttermilk

Preparation:
Mix the salt with the flour
Then mix in the butter (use a mixer)
Separately mix the buttermilk, sugar and eggs
Mix it in with the flour
If necessary soften the mixture with milk
It will form bread like dough
Smear butter inside bread baking pans completely covering them
Divide and place the dough in the bread baking pans
The dough should only be a ¼ of the height inside of the bread baking pans
Bake in the oven at 350° F for about 20 minutes until done
Remove from the oven and allow to cool
Cut in 2 inch slices and then cut each slice 3 inches wide
Place them in the oven and bake them at 200° F for about 3 hours to dry
Leave the oven door slightly open for the moisture to escape
Be careful not to burn them
Then remove from the oven and allow cooling
Place in a closed container and enjoy
When eating dunk them in hot coffee or tea
Be careful not to burn your mouth when eating
Should last up to 6 months

Basic Acorn Recipes
Acorns may be used as grits
Acorn grits may be deep fried and eaten as a side dish
Acorn grits may be added to soups or salads
Acorn grits may be fried briefly in a skillet and used as an ingredient of granola
Acorn meal may be used in most recipes for ¼ of the flour or a ¼ of the corn meal
100% Acorn Bread will be hard if baked too long or crumbly if not baked long enough

Indian Acorn Griddlecakes
Ingredients:
> 2 cups of Acorn meal
> ¾ cup of water
> ½ tsp of salt

Preparation:
Combine everything and beat to a stiff batter
Allow to stand for one hour
Heat 1 tbsp of fat or oil in frying pan
Carefully place a large spoon of acorn batter into a pan to form each cake
Brown slowly on both sides
Serve
Will keep for about 4 days

Mexican Acorn Tortilla
Ingredients:
> 2 cups of acorn meal
> ¾ cup of flour
> 2 tsp of salt
> Preparation:
> Mix the ingredients
> Add just enough water to make stiff dough
> Let it stand for 40 minutes
> Form into 3 inch diameter balls and then flatten each ball to ¼ inch thick
> Fry each one in a lightly greased skillet until brown on both sides
> Serve

Living in Difficult Times

Pemmican Acorn Tortillas
Ingredients:
    ½ cup of fine ground acorn meal
    1 lb of finely ground meat
    Several tortillas

Preparation:
Boil the meat in salted water until tender
Drain and allow to dry
Mix the meat with the acorn meal
(Add cooked rice, cooked beans, hot sauce or grated cheese
if desired)
Season to taste
Heat and serve wrapped in a tortilla, or on any flatbread

Acorn Bread
Ingredients:
    1 cup of acorn meal
    1 cup of flour
    1 egg
    1 tsp of salt
    3 tbsp of baking soda
    3 tbsp of oil
    1 cup of milk or water

Preparation:
Combine the milk, egg, oil and beat until smooth
Mix in the acorn meal, flour, salt, and baking soda and stir
into a smooth dough
Form and place in a greased bread pan
Bake at 400° F for 30 minutes
Serve

Acorn Muffins
    Use the same above recipe
    Use a greased muffin pan and fill each space (2/3 full)
      with the above mixture
    Bake at 400° F for 20 minutes and serve

Acorn Pancakes
Preparation:
Use the above recipe, but use 2 eggs and 1¼ cups of milk
This will provide a softer batter
Carefully place the batter into a hot oiled pan (enough to make a pancake)
When brown, turn and brown the other side
Serve with butter, cream, syrup, honey, jam or fresh fruit

Breakfast Acorn meal (Similar to Oatmeal)
Ingredients:
    1 cup of acorn meal
    2½ cups of water
    1/8 cup of crushed nuts
    1 tsp of salt
    1 tsp of honey or sugar

Preparation:
Boil the water adding the salt
Add the acorn meal and continue boiling for 20 minutes
Turn off heat
Let cool for five minutes
Stir in the honey, sugar and nuts
Serve

Acorn and Corn Meal Mush
Ingredients:
    1 cup of acorn meal
    5 cups of water
    2 cups of corn meal
    1 tsp of salt

Preparation:
Bring the water in a pot to a boil adding the salt
Sprinkle the acorn meal slowly into the boiling water and stir continuously
Then add the corn meal when the mixture starts to bubble
If too thick, add water
If too thin, add cornmeal

Simmer in a closed pot for about 50 minutes, stirring until it becomes thick
Serve hot

It may be served with:
    Milk and sugar,
    Butter and sugar, or
    Grated cheese and bacon bits
or
Form the mush into a loaf in a pan and place in the refrigerator for about 10 hours
Remove from the pan and slice it with a knife into ½ inch thick slices
Fry each side in a heated, oiled skillet
Serve with butter, cream, syrup or jam

Acorn Bread
Ingredients:
    2 cups of acorn meal
    ½ cup of milk or water
    1 tbsp of baking soda
    2 cups of flour
    2 tbsp of oil or butter
    1 egg
    Optional Sweeteners: Add 1/3 cup of honey, maple syrup or sugar

Preparation:
Combine all the ingredients into a loaf pan
Bake at 400ºF for 35 minutes or until done
Serve

Glazed Acorn Treats
Ingredients:
    Shelled, boiled, washed and dried acorns (See method –
    page 112)
    4 cups of sugar
    1 tsp of salt
    ¼ tsp of cream of tartar
    2 cups of water

Preparation:
Mix and dissolve the sugar, salt and cream of tartar in 2 cups of water
Bring it to a boil in a pot until it shows signs of browning
Place the pot in a larger pot of boiling water to keep it in a liquid state
(Or use a double boiler)
Dip each individual acorn into the mixture
Place on a sheet of wax paper to dry and harden
Enjoy the next day

Acorn Cookies
Ingredients:
2½ cups of flour
1½ cups of ground acorns
1 cup of sugar
1 tsp of baking soda
¾ cup of butter
1 egg
1 tsp of vanilla extract (or any other extract of your choice)
1 tsp of salt

Preparation:
Combine the flour, baking soda and salt
Separately mix the butter and the sugar in a bowl
Mix in the egg and vanilla extract
Then blend in the dry ingredients gradually and then the ground acorns
Divide the dough into small pieces and roll into balls
Place on a lightly greased baking sheet and flatten
Bake at 350°F for 15 minutes or until done
Remove and allow to cool and serve

Chestnuts
How to roast
Always make slits on the chestnuts, to break the tough skin
Do this along the rounded side of each chestnut
This will prevent them from popping during cooking

Living in Difficult Times

Roasting over an open fire
Place one layer in a grill basket
Move or shake them frequently back and forth over the fire while grilling
Do not let them char
When the skins have been blackened by the heat, they should be done

On a stovetop
Place just one layer in a pan over medium heat and sprinkle them with water
Shake the pan back and forth frequently
Prevent them from charring
When the skins have been blackened by the heat, they should be done
This usually takes up to 10 minutes

In the microwave
Always make slits on the chestnuts, to break the tough skin
Do this along the rounded side of each chestnut
This will prevent them from popping
Place 8 raw chestnuts on a dish and cook them for about 40 seconds at full power

Boiling chestnuts
Slit the raw chestnuts, and boil them for 12 minutes
Take them out of the water and shell them

Chestnut paste
Shell and boil the raw chestnuts for about 12 minutes
Crush the chestnuts in a kitchen cloth while hot, to break their crisp skins
Remove the fur-like skin and blend the nuts to make a paste

Chestnut lasagne
Make lasagne sheets (see recipe below)
Place the lasagne sheets at the bottom of an oven proof dish
Layer it with a mixture of cream mushroom soup, meat and greens
Add more lasagne sheets to cover it
Layer it again with a mixture of cream mushroom soup, meat and greens
Repeat this layer for layer to fill the dish
Bake in an oven at 350° F for 35 minutes
Sprinkle the top with cheese, bake up to 16 minutes until done and serve

How to make lasagne sheets
Ingredients:
    4 cups of chestnut flour (or regular flour)
    5 eggs
    2 tbsp of cooking oil
    1 tsp of salt
    Enough water

Preparation:
Place the chestnut flour in a large bowl
At the centre add the eggs, cooking oil and salt
Mix slowly adding more flour from the edges
Knead the dough until you obtain smooth dough
Adjust with small quantities of flour or water as needed
Form a ball with the dough
Let it rest for about 1 hour covered with a moist cloth
Roll out the dough to obtain flat sheets that will cook evenly
Keep the sheets separated to avoid them from sticking together
In a skillet add 1 tablespoon of cooking oil to water
Bring it to a boil and then add salt
Then place the lasagne sheets briefly in boiling water before using them
Oil will keep the squares from sticking together

Living in Difficult Times

Dairy products
Milk:

> *Rice milk*
> 8 cups of hot water
> 2 cups of cooked white rice
> 2 tsp of vanilla extract
> Place all ingredients in a blender until smooth
> Set for about 40 minutes without shaking
> Pour off the milk leaving the sediment in the first container
> Use the liquid and refrigerate

Coconut milk
(Not the liquid inside a coconut)
Mix the grated flesh of a coconut with some hot water
Set aside for 10 minutes and squeeze out the milk
Do not shake and it will separate into two layers
The thick (upper) layer is the coconut cream
The thin (bottom) layer is the milk
Use and refrigerate
or
Empty a 16 oz packet of grated coconut into a blender and add 2 cups of boiling water
Blend for a minute and allow the mixture to cool
Squeeze out the milk
Use within 2 days and refrigerate

Sweetened condensed milk
Ingredients:
> 1¼ cups of dry milk powder
> ½ cup of warm water
> ¾ cup of sugar

Preparation:
Mix the warm water and dry milk in a dish
Stir in the sugar slowly
Set the dish in a pan of hot water to dissolve the sugar
Use it as condensed milk

Sour Cream
Ingredients:
    2½ cups of dry milk
    1 cup of warm water
    2 tablespoons of vinegar

Preparation:
Mix the warm water and dry milk powder
Stir in the vinegar a few drops at a time until smooth
Allow to thicken in the refrigerator for several hours and use

Butter
Regular butter
or
Refrigerated olive oil that will congeal as butter

Spreadable margarine
Mix 2 sticks of butter with 1 cup of corn oil and refrigerate
It will last up to a month

Animal fats - rendered
Heat the fat trimmings from meat cuts, separating the fat mixture from the solids
The separated fat may be poured off and used in food products, or soap making
Rendered pure animal fat may also be used in frying, cooking or spread on bread

Egg substitute
Mix 8 tbsp of ground flaxseed with 1½ cups of water
Simmer in a pan until a thick egg-like consistency has been reached
Allow to cool before using in a recipe

Cheese:
Cheddar cheese
Ingredients:
   1 Gallon of fresh milk
   1 oz of Mesophilic starter culture
   ¼ tablet of Rennet
   1 tbsp of Salt

Preparation:
Warm the milk to 90°F in a double boiler
Add the Mesophilic starter culture and mix thoroughly
Allow to set for one hour
Dissolve the ¼ tablet of rennet into 4 tablespoons of cold water
Slowly pour the mixture into the milk stirring constantly for 6 minutes
Set aside for about 2 hours until a firm curd has formed
Slice the curd every ½ inch with a knife in both directions to form squares
Allow the curds to sit for 20 minutes to firm up
Then heat and slowly raise the temperature to 102° F (takes about 50 minutes)
During this time, gently stir the curds every few minutes so they don't mat together
Now continue to cook the curds at 102° F for another 50 minutes
During this time, gently stir the curds every few minutes so they don't mat together
Line a colander with cheesecloth
Pour the curds through it to drain away the whey (watery mix)
Don't allow the curds to mat
Place the curds back into the double boiler at 102° F
Stir the curds to separate any matted particles
Add a tablespoon of salt and mix thoroughly
Now cook the curds at 102° F for one hour, stirring every few minutes
Place the curds into a cheese press lined with cheese cloth

Press the cheese at about 20 lbs pressure for 50 minutes
Remove the cheese from the press and flip it around
Press the cheese at about 40 lbs pressure for 3 hours
Remove the cheese from the press and flip it around
Press the cheese at about 50 lbs pressure for 26 hours
Remove the cheese from the press
Place the cheese on a board at room temperature for about 6 days
The cheese should be dry to the touch
Age the cheese in a refrigerator for at least 3 months
Flip the cheese every three days
After 4 weeks place a red edible wax coating over the cheese
It will have an extended life of a year or longer

Gouda Cheese
Ingredients:
1 Gallon of Fresh Milk
4 oz of Mesophilic Starter Culture
¼ tablet of Rennet
Preparation:
Warm the milk to 85° F
Add the Mesophilic starter culture and mix thoroughly
Dissolve ¼ tablet of rennet into 4 tablespoons of cold water
Slowly pour the rennet into the milk stirring constantly for about 6 minutes
Allow the milk to set for 2 hours until a firm curd is set
Slice the curd every ½ inch with a knife in both directions to form squares
Allow the curds to firm for 15 minutes
Slowly raise the temperature to 102° F (takes about 50 minutes)
Stir the curds every few minutes so they don't mat together and allow them to settle
Carefully remove 3 cups of whey from the surface
Replace the removed whey with 3 cups of 102° F water
Cook the curds at 102° F for another 60 minutes
Every 20 minutes remove 3 cups of whey and replace with 102° F water
Do this three times

Living in Difficult Times

Line a colander with cheesecloth
Pour the curds through the cheesecloth
Place the drained curds into a cheese press
Press the cheese at about 20 lbs for 50 minutes
Remove the cheese from the press and flip it around
Press the cheese at about 40 lbs for 3 hours
Carefully remove the cheese from the press

Place the cheese for 3½ hours in a cold brine solution
Flip the cheese around every 50 minutes
Pat the cheese dry until the outer surface begins to harden

Place it in a covered container in the refrigerator, for 4 weeks
Flip the cheese around every day
Inspect it every day for mould
Wipe off any mould with a paper towel dipped in white vinegar
Continue to flip it around every 3 days
Wax after 4 weeks with a edible red cheese wax
It will have an extended life of a year or longer

Brine solution
Dissolve 1½ cups of salt into a quart of warm water
Cool the brine in your refrigerator and use

Cottage cheese
Ingredients:
    2 cups of dry milk
    ½ cup of buttermilk
    ½ gallon of water
    ½ gallon of boiling water
    Large container
    Large pot

Preparation:
Mix the dry milk with ½ gallon of water in a large dish
Add ½ cup of buttermilk
Place the dish of mixture in a pot of hot water to coagulate quickly
Cut the curd into ½ cubes in both directions with a knife
Pour ½ gallon of boiling water over the mixture and let it stand

Then squeeze the curd between two fingers so as to show a fingerprint
Then it is ready to wash out
Wash out all the whey with cold water and drain
Season to taste with salt and cream

Cream Cheese (vegetarian)

Ingredients: 2 cups macadamia nuts, soaked for 8 hours, then rinsed and drained
2 cups of pine nuts, soaked for 4 hours, then rinsed and drained
½ cup of lemon juice
4 tsp of maple syrup
2 tsp of salt
Water
Preparation:
Place nuts, lemon juice and maple syrup and blend in blender
Slowly add water to create a creamy consistency
Enjoy

Dessert

Yogurt and frozen yogurt

Ingredients:
2 pints of milk
2 tablespoons of existing yogurt
Preparation:
Use two pots that fit inside one another (as a double boiler)
Place water in the outer pot
Place the milk in the inner pot and keep stirring
Boil the water in the outer pot to 185° F
Then place the pot of milk in a pot of cold water stirring it occasionally
Cool the milk to 110° F
Add 2 tablespoons of the existing yogurt which is at room temperature
Pour it into a clean container and tightly cover with a lid
Keep the yogurt warm at 100° F for 7 to 8 hours to incubate

It will look like custard, smell like cheese and have a greenish liquid on top
Remove the greenish liquid
Enjoy the yogurt
Use yogurt from this batch as starter for the next batch

Optional flavours
Mix -
4 cups of yogurt
1 cup of sugar
Vanilla or any other flavour
2 tablespoons of existing yogurt

Refrigerate the yogurt for several hours until cold
It will keep for 7 days
If a thin yellow liquid forms on the top (whey), stir it in before eating the yogurt

Ice cream
Ingredients:
> 10 egg yolks
> 2 cups of sugar
> 1 cup of milk
> 1 cup of cream
> 4 tablespoons of butter
> 2 cups of whipped cream
> 4 tsp of vanilla or other extract
> Food colouring for ice-cream colour of your choice

Preparation:
Beat the egg yolks, sugar and blend in a pot
Place the pot in another pot of water (double boiler)
Stir in the milk and cream and bring the pot of water to a boil
Cook and stir the mixture until it thickens
Take out the pot, set it aside and stir in the butter to the mixture
Let it cool, stirring it occasionally until it reaches room temperature

Stir in whipping cream and vanilla or other extract
Stir in food colouring, freeze and serve

Making gelatine powder

Kudzu roots
Kudzu Roots 1½ inches thick should be harvested December through March
Wash the roots and cut them into 1 inch slices
Puree in a blender with enough cold water
Strain and squeeze to extract all the liquid
The brown kudzu liquid should be filtered through a cotton fabric
It should be left in a cool place for 24 hours
The brown liquid should be poured off and a clay like substance will remain
Break it up and mix it well with clean water once again
Allow it to rest for 24 hours in a cool environment
The brown liquid should again be poured off and a clay like substance will remain
Break it up and mix it well with clean water once again,
Allow it to rest for 48 hours in a cool environment
Pour off the brown liquid and keep the substance (starch) that remains
The starch is ready to be used immediately or can be dried for later use
To dry the kudzu starch, place it on a tray or on layers of paper
Set it in a cool, ventilated place for 10 or more days until dry
Pulverize the dry chunks of kudzu starch into powder and store in a sealed container

Knobby Greenbrier roots (Smilax)
Wash the roots and cut them into 1 inch slices
Puree in a blender with cold water
Strain and squeeze to extract all the liquid
The liquid should be filtered through a cotton fabric

It should be left in a cool place for 24 hours
The liquid should be poured off and a substance (Starch) will remain
The starch is ready to be used immediately or can be dried for later use
To dry the starch, place it on a tray or on layers of paper
Set it in a cool, ventilated place for 10 or more days until dry
Pulverize the dry chunks of starch into powder and store in a sealed container

Making Jelly
Ingredients:
1½ tablespoons of gelatine
2 cups of water
1¼ cups of fruit juice (or flavouring)
1 cup of sugar

Preparation:
Combine 1 cup cold water with gelatine powder in a bowl and set aside
Combine the sugar and juice (or flavouring) in another bowl
Boil 1 cup of water
Remove it from the heat and add the sugar and juice mixture
Pour the hot mixture into the water and gelatine
Refrigerate up to 3 hours until the jelly is firm

Custard
Heat 4 cups of milk
Whisk 6 eggs until smooth and add them to the milk
Add 3 cups of sugar
Add salt and vanilla until it dissolves (to taste)
Pour into a baking dish and bake at 325° F for about 30 minutes
Insert a knife in the centre and if it comes out clean it is done
Cool before serving

Bread pudding
Ingredients:
1 loaf of bread
4 tablespoons of butter
6 eggs
4 cups of milk
2 cups of sugar
2 tbsp of cinnamon
2 teaspoons of vanilla
¾ cup of raisins

Preparation:
Preheat the oven to 350° F
Grease a casserole dish
Cut the loaf of bread into small cubes
Toss together the bread cubes and raisins in the casserole dish
Whip together melted butter, eggs, milk, sugar, cinnamon and vanilla
Pour the liquid mixture over the bread cubes and raisins
Bake the pudding for about 50 minutes until set
Serve

Potato pancakes
Ingredients:
1 cup milk
2 tbsp of cooking oil
1 tbsp of active dry yeast
4 crushed cloves of garlic
Salt and pepper to taste
1 cup of potatoes
6 cups of flour

Preparation:
Blend the lukewarm milk, oil, yeast, garlic, pepper and salt in a blender
Add the potatoes and blend until finely chopped
Mix the flour with the dry yeast separately

Living in Difficult Times

Mix it with the blended liquid
Shape round pancakes, ½ thick
Close with a cloth in a warm place for 1 hour to rise
Brown for up to 8 minutes on each side in a frying pan
Serve

Fruit pie shell
(May be used with all the pies)
Ingredients:
2½ cups of flour
½ tsp of salt
1 cup of margarine
1/3 cup of cold water

Preparation:
Mix the flour and salt in large bowl
Mix in about 2/3 of the cup of margarine into the flour
It should create a texture like cornmeal
Cut in the rest of the margarine until it crumbs the size of peas
Sprinkle 1 tablespoon of water at a time over the mixture
Mix it with a fork until the particles stick together
(Too much water will make the pie crust dough sticky.
Too little water will make the dough crumbly and hard to work with)
Gently form a ball by pressing the particles together
Wrap the ball in plastic wrap and refrigerate for 40 minutes
Divide the ball of dough in half
(One for the bottom pie crust and the other for the top)
Sprinkle a flat work surface lightly with flour
Flatten the ball of dough gently to ½ inch thick and sprinkle the top with flour
Roll with a floured rolling pin from centre to the edge of the dough, in all directions
The circle of dough should be about 2 inches wider than the pie pan
It should cover the bottom and sides of the pan.
Make a second one to cover the top of the pie

Different fruit pies

Elderberry pie
Ingredients:
- 3½ cups of apples
- 1 cup of honey
- 3 spoons of ground spicebush berries
- 2 cups of elderberries
- 2 tbsp of melted butter
- 1 tbsp of lemon or lime juice

Preparation:
Place ingredients into an unbaked pie shell
Then cover with 2 cups of elderberries
Sprinkle with melted butter
Add the top pie shell
Make two slits in the top of the crust and bake at 350° F for 35 minutes until brown
Serve
See pie shell recipe above

Apple pie
Ingredients:
- 1 cup of sugar
- ½ cup of flour
- ½ tsp of ground nutmeg
- 1 tsp of ground cinnamon
- Salt to taste
- 9 cups of peeled, cored and sliced apples
- 3 tablespoons of melted butter

Preparation:
Heat oven to 425° F
Mix sugar, flour, nutmeg, cinnamon and salt in bowl
Stir in the apples
Pour into an unbaked pie shell
Sprinkle with the melted butter
Cover with the top piecrust and seal the edges

Cut two slits in the top of the piecrust
Bake at 350° F for 35 minutes or until slightly brown
Juice will begin to bubble through slits at the top and serve
See pie shell recipe above

Cherry pie
2 lbs of tart cherries with the juice
1½ cups of sugar
½ tsp of almond extract
Salt to taste
2 tbsp of melted butter

Preparation:
Mix the cherries, sugar, almond extract, salt and pour into an
unbaked pie shell
Sprinkle the melted butter over the top
Cover with the top crust, seal the edges and cut two slits in it
Bake at 375° F for 35 minutes or until slightly brown
(See pie shell recipe above)

Blackberry pie
Ingredients:
3 cups of blackberries
1½ cups of sugar
2 cups of water
½ cup of cornstarch
¾ cup of water

Preparation:
Mix the blackberries, sugar, 2 cups of water and boil for 12
minutes
Add cornstarch to ¾ cup of water and stir well
Pour it into the cooked berries and it will thicken
Pour the mixture into an unbaked pie shell
Cover with top crust and seal the edges
Cut two slits in the top of the piecrust
Bake at 375° F until slightly brown
See pie shell recipe above

Blueberry pie
Ingredients:
   4 cups of blueberries
   1 cup of sugar
   ¼ cup of lemon juice
   1/3 cup of cornstarch
   ½ cup of water

Preparation:
Mix together the blueberries, sugar, lemon juice in a pot over medium heat
Bring to a boil, stirring frequently
Mix cornstarch with the water to make a paste
Pour it into the blueberry mixture, stirring until it thickens
Remove it from the heat and let it cool
Pour the blueberry mixture into an unbaked pie shell
Cover with top crust and seal the edges
Cut two slits in the top of the piecrust and bake at 375° F until slightly brown
See pie shell recipe above

Brownies
Ingredients:
   1¾ cups of flour
   ¼ cup of acorn flour
   1 cup of chopped walnuts
   1 cup of honey
   ¾ cup of water
   1 tsp of baking soda

Preparation:
Mix the water and baking soda
Mix it into the other ingredients
Then pour in a greased pan and bake at 350° F for about 50 minutes
Cool, cut and serve

Baking a cake
In 2 cake pans (9 inch)
Ingredients:
    2 cups of cake flour
    2 tsp of baking powder
    1 cup of sugar
    ½ tsp of salt
    ½ cup of soft butter
    4 medium eggs (at room temperature)
    2 teaspoons of vanilla extract (or other)
    ¾ cup of milk

Preparation:
Preheat the oven to 350° F
Grease and flour the cake pans
Mix the flour, baking powder and salt in a bowl
Whisk in butter and sugar until it becomes light
Beat in one egg at a time
Mix in the vanilla
Mix in the milk until smooth
Divide into 2 pans
Bake at 350° F for about 30 minutes
Cool for 10 minutes
Carefully remove from the pans
Add about ½ inch thick frosting or jam on the top of one of the cakes
Carefully place the second cake on top of the frosting or jam
Now frost the whole cake (top and sides if desired)

Making icing used for Frosting
Ingredients:
    3 cups of icing sugar (sugar that is ground to powder)
    ¼ cup of margarine
    ¼ cup of cream
    1 tsp of Vanilla extract

Preparation:
Mix margarine, cream and bring to a boil
Mix in the icing sugar and vanilla to smooth or drizzle over the cake

Drinks

Lemonade:

Sumac red berries
(White sumac berries are poisonous.)
Pick the red berries in late summer and place them in a jar of boiling water
Allow them to sit for about one minute (do not use a strong concentration)
Strain
Sweeten the liquid to taste

Red clover blossoms
Soak in water
Add sugar
Strain and serve

Elderberry flowers
Soak flowers in cold water
Add sugar to taste
Add vinegar to taste
Let stand for 24 hours
Strain and simmer for 25 minutes
Cool and serve

Grape-like drink
Kudzu flowers
Steep them in water
(Use more flowers for a stronger taste)
Sweeten to taste
Cool and serve

Living in Difficult Times

Passion fruit drink
Open and remove the seeds
Cut and place in a blender
Add water and blend
Cool and serve
Has a fruity taste

Tea
(Simmer each of these different kinds of ingredients separately.
Each produces a unique taste of tea)
- Yarrow flowers
- Agrimony dried leaves
- Dried Bergamot tops when flowering
- Red clover blossoms
- Dandelion petals
- Plantain leaves
- Rose hips
- Spicebush leaves and twigs
- Sweet birch twigs – (it produces a pink colour tea)
- Goldenrod lance leaves – (it produces a gold colour
  tea, used as a health tonic)
- Blue Violet flowers – (it produces a purple colour tea)
- Sassafras leaves and pieces of cut sassafras root
  (Remove dirt, peel the root, cut into pieces and steep to
  the desired strength.
  Do not boil as boiling will produce a bitter taste)
  Sweeten to taste and serve

Coffee choices
Use individually or combine the ingredients according to taste
Clean, dry and oven roast them until they are brown
Grind and use as ground coffee
- Chicory root
- Beechnuts
- Dandelion roots
- Chufa tubers (autumn or spring)
- Juniper berries
- Combination of chicory, dandelion and beet roots

Coffey - roasting
Wash the chicory root thoroughly to remove all the soil
Slice the root into ¼ inch pieces
Slice the thicker part of the root to maintain the same width
Arrange them in a single layer on a cookie sheet
Place in a pre-heated oven and roast at 325° F until golden brown and dry
(Up to 80 minutes)
Remove from the oven and allow to dry overnight
Grind to a Coffey powder, enjoy and store

Chocolate -
Roots of a Water Aven may be cleaned, dried, roasted and ground
Use as a form of chocolate drink

Beer
Birch sap tapped from birch trees and fermented to become a beer

Pineapple beer
Cut up 3 Pineapples (including the skin)
Place the pieces in 1 gallon of water
Add 4 cups of sugar
Allow to ferment for a 4 days and then refrigerate and serve

Cornmeal beer
Ingredients:
1 cup of fine corn meal
10 cups of powdered malt (if necessary grind and sift it to obtain a powder)
2½ cups of water

Preparation:
Boil the water in a pot
Stir in the corn meal and cook it until a soft porridge is formed
Remove from the heat, allow it to cool and then stir in the malt

The mixture should have a pourable consistency (If too thick, add water)
Add sugar to taste and leave covered for 24 hours to ferment
Serve.

Snacks

Chicken skin rinds
Fry chicken skins in boiling oil for several minutes until they become crisp
(Be careful to avoid burns)
Or
Microwave them for a few minutes

Hard baked bagels
Bagels broken in pieces
Then dipped in honey mustard sauce and dried
Serve

Seeds popped like popcorn in a microwave

Seeds dried and eaten
Sunflower, pumpkin, squash and fruit seeds

Raisons
Grapes dehydrated or placed on a flat shallow pan and sun dried

Dried fruit
Fruit dehydrated or placed on a flat shallow pan and sun dried

Nuts of various kinds

Dried vegetables
Vegetables sliced thinly, dehydrated or placed on a flat shallow pan and sun dried

Potato chips
Potatoes thinly sliced, chilled and then gently placed in boiling oil
(Be careful to avoid burns)
Seasoned, cooled and served

Candy

Chocolate and nut fudge
Ingredients:
    5 chocolate squares (candy-making)
    ½ cup of water
    ½ cup of cream
    2 tbsp butter
    1 cup of sugar
    1 cup of brown sugar
    ½ tsp of salt
    1 tsp vanilla extract
    1 cup of broken nuts

Preparation:
Blend and heat the water and cream
Stir in the sugar and salt and bring to a boil
Remove from the heat and add the butter
Allow to cool and add the vanilla
Beat until it thickens and add the nuts
Continue beating until it loses its gloss
Lightly grease a small shallow pan (9 by 4 inches)
Pour the mixture into it
Allow to cool and refrigerate
Cut into squares
Enjoy

Nut brittle
Ingredients:
　　1 cup of corn syrup
　　2 cups of sugar
　　½ cup of water
　　2 cups of peanuts
　　1½ tsp of salt
　　1 tsp of vanilla extract
　　¾ tsp of baking soda
　　4 tbsp of butter

Preparation:
Melt 2 tbsp butter in a pan
Cover with nuts
Separately heat syrup and water to 350° F and pour over the nuts
Add 2 tbsp butter, vanilla extract, and stir until the butter melts
Sprinkle the baking soda over the surface of the mixture and stir
As it begins to foam it will double in volume
Pour the mixture onto a clean baking sheet and it will quickly harden
Allow it to cool and then break it into pieces
Enjoy

Pecan, Hickory and Beechnuts caramelized
Pour maple syrup about ½ inches deep into a 10 inch non-stick skillet
Bring to a boil over high heat
When the syrup begins to bubble, add the nuts and stir them in to coat them
Immediately scoop them out onto a flat surface pan to cool
When cold break them apart
Enjoy

Toasted nuts
Mix 2 cups of shelled nuts with 1 cup of melted butter
Toast them in an oven at 375° F
When they are a dark brown colour remove them from the oven
Salt and season to taste

Orange rinds candy
Ingredients:
>   5 oranges
>   2 cups of sugar
>   1 cup of cold water

Preparation:
Wash and dry the oranges
Peel the oranges and remove the white pith
Cut the peels in 3 inch long strips about ½ inch wide
Boil and strain them to remove bitterness (possible twice)
Heat 1 cup of water and dissolve 1 cup of sugar in it
Add the orange rinds and simmer until they are translucent
Remove and toss them with 1 cup of sugar
Separate and place them on a rack to dry
Place in a closed container and enjoy up to 10 days

Lemon Gum drops
Ingredients:
>   1 cup of lemon juice
>   2 oz of fruit pectin
>   ½ tsp of baking soda
>   3 cups of sugar
>   1 cup of corn syrup

Preparation:
Boil lemon juice, pectin and baking soda
Keep on low heat and keep stirring
Add sugar and corn syrup to a separate pot reaching 285° F
Slowly pour it into the hot juice mixture
Allow it to stand for 3 minutes removing any foam

Living in Difficult Times

Line a bread baking pan with foil
Lightly coat it with margarine
Pour the candy mixture into it
Allow it to rest overnight at normal temperature
Remove the foil from the pan and cut into 1 inch squares
Roll them in sugar, allow to rest for 2 hours and refrigerate
Store them in a closed container
Enjoy

Chewing gum
Break off sap that has come out of cuts in the bark of a Sweet gum tree
Use as gum

Condiments and taste enhancers

Taco Sauce
Ingredients:
- 6 oz of tomato paste
- 3 cups of water
- 2 tsp of cayenne pepper
- 2 tsp of chilli powder
- 2 tsp of salt
- 2 tsp of cornstarch
- 2½ tsp of white vinegar
- 2 tbsp of minced dried onions
- 1 small hot pepper

Directions:
- Combine the tomato paste with the water in a large pan over medium heat
- Stir until smooth
- Add the cayenne, chilli powder, salt, cornstarch and vinegar
- Puree the onion and hot pepper until smooth
- Add this to the tomato, water mixture and stir while bringing it to a boil

After 4 minutes, remove it from the heat and allow it to cool
Seal it in a container and refrigerate
It may be canned or used for about 40 days

Imitation Avocado spread
Ingredients:
  3 cups of spinach
  ½ cup of cooking oil (more oil to thicken the spread)
  1 tsp of Basil
  1 tbsp of lemon juice
  2 tbsp of vinegar
  Salt & pepper to taste

Preparation:
Blend the spinach adding the oil slowly and then the other ingredients
Serve the blended paste with chips or crackers

Vegetable or cracker Dip
Edible greens and flowers finely chopped and blended with sour cream
Seasoned to taste
Serve

Ketchup
Ingredients:
  12 lbs of very ripe tomatoes
  3 large chopped onions
  2 chopped green peppers
  2 cloves of garlic
  2 cups of sugar
  2 cups of vinegar
  1 tbsp of paprika
  1 tbsp of dry mustard
  Salt and pepper to taste

Utensils: A large saucepan, a strainer, canning jars and lids
Preparation:
Add to a large pot and cook the following for 50 minutes until tender
(Tomatoes, onions, green peppers, garlic, sugar, vinegar, salt, paprika and dry mustard powder)
Strain out the tomato peels and seeds
Simmer and stir over low heat for 2½ hours, until the mixture is thick
Sterilize the jars before filling them
Fill them completely with the hot ketchup and immediately close them
When they cool they will seal
Store them in a dark, cool place
Enjoy

Mayonnaise
Ingredients:
   3 egg yolks
   2 tbsp of mustard
   Salt and pepper to taste
   16 oz of cooking oil (more oil to thicken the Mayonnaise)
   1 tbsp of vinegar

Preparation:
Bring all the ingredients to room temperature
Combine the egg yolk, mustard, salt, pepper in a bowl and whisk
Continue whisking and adding 5 fl oz of oil in drops, until the mayonnaise emulsifies
Then slowly whisk in the remaining oil until the mayonnaise is smooth and thick
Then whisk in the vinegar
Add the seasoning to taste
Enjoy

Peanut butter
Blend the nuts in a blender until it becomes a soft paste (any nuts of your choice)
Enjoy

Jam
Ingredients:
>   4 pounds of fresh strawberries (or other sliced fruit of your choice)
>   8 cups of sugar (adjust the amount of sugar with other fruit used)
>   ½ cup of lemon juice

Preparation:
Place the strawberries or fruit in a pot
Mix in the sugar and lemon juice
Stir over a low heat until the sugar is dissolved and then bring to a boil
Keep stirring
Test the mixture by dipping a spoon in it
As you take the spoon out, droplets will drop off it
If it drops in a steady stream – it is not ready
If it drops quickly, drop by drop – it is ready
(If boiled too long it will harden when it cools)
Remove from the heat and bottle
Refrigerate and enjoy

Apple butter
Peel, core and slice 3 lbs of tart apples
Cook them in 3 cups of apple cider in an iron pot for 25 minutes
Blend in a blender and cook for another 25 minutes
Add 1½ cups of sugar
Add 1 tsp on cinnamon
Add ½ tsp of cloves
Add ½ tsp of all spice
Stir and boil for about I hour to desired thickness
Remove from the heat and bottle
Refrigerate
Otherwise can it in jars
Enjoy

Tartar sauce
1 cup of mayonnaise
4 tbsp of ground sweet pickle relish
2 tsp of dill
Mix well and refrigerate
Enjoy

Soy sauce (imitation)
Ingredients:
Juice of 2 lemons
7 tbsp of oil
7 tbsp of water
2½ tsp of oriental five spice powder (see recipe below)
½ tsp of sesame seed oil
½ cup of sugar
½ tsp of ginger
¼ teaspoon of ground black pepper
Preparation:
Mix the ingredients
Enjoy

Oriental five spice powder (imitation)
Combine the following ingredients:
4 tbsp of anise seed
4 tbsp of fennel
8 tsp of ground cinnamon
2 tsp of pepper
1 tsp of ground cloves
Enjoy

Old Bay seasoning (imitation)
Combine the following ingredients and enjoy:
4 tbsp of ground bay leaves
4 tbsp celery salt
2 tbsp dry mustard
4 tsp of ground black pepper
4 tsp of ground ginger
4 tsp of sweet paprika

2 tsp of ground pepper
2 tsp of ground nutmeg
2 tsp of ground cloves
2 tsp of ground allspice

Curry powder
Ingredients:
4 tbsp of cumin seeds
4 tbsp of cardamom seeds
4 tbsp coriander seeds
1 tbsp of fennel seeds
6 tbsp of ground turmeric
1 tbsp of cinnamon
2 tbsp of ground ginger
2 tbsp of dry mustard
2 tsp of chilli powder
4 tsp of garlic powder
½ tsp of white pepper

Preparation:
Heat a skillet to medium heat
Add the cumin, cardamom, and coriander seeds
Toast the seeds stirring constantly for 1 minute until fragrant
Remove skillet and allow it to cool
Pour the ingredients into a bowl and stir in the remaining spices
Then grind them in a grinder to a fine curry powder
Pour the curry powder through a fine sieve
Keep in an air-tight glass jar, in a cool dry place and make curry dishes

Creole mix
Combine the following ingredients:
4 tsp of onion powder
4 tsp of garlic powder
4 tsp of dried oregano leaves
4 tsp of dried sweet basil leaves

2 tsp of dried thyme leaves
2 tsp of pepper
2 tsp of cayenne pepper
10 tsp of sweet paprika
Enjoy

Teriyaki sauce
Ingredients:
1 cup of soy sauce
1 cup of wine
4 tbsp of sugar

Preparation:
Mix and stir all ingredients in a pan at low heat and simmer for 4 minutes
Remove from the heat and cool
Bottle, refrigerate and enjoy

Sugar meat cure – for about 40 lbs of meat
8 cups of salt
1½ cups of brown sugar
4 tbsp of black pepper
½ tsp of red pepper
½ tsp of salt peter
Mix the ingredients and rub on the meat

Relishes

Burdock pickles
Ingredients:
8 cups of burdock root (or onions and vegetables)
Cut into finger-size pieces
2 cups of vinegar
2 cups of water
4 tbsp of allspice
4 tbsp of bayberry leaves
2 tbsp of anise

4 tbsp of fresh ground ginger
4 tsp of black mustard seeds
2 tsp of cloves
2 tsp of salt

Preparation:
Steam the burdock (or vegetables) for 35 minutes until tender
Drain and put into canning jars
Mix the vinegar and the water in a pot and bring it to a boil
Add the remaining ingredients
Pour and spoon it into hot canning jars containing the burdock (vegetables)
Leave about a 1/8 inch of space at the top
Place canning lids on jars
Tighten and turn the jars upside down so that all the heat is on the seals
Turn them back upright once the jars are completely cool
Refrigerate and begin to serve the next day
Enjoy

Corn relish
Ingredients:
10 cups of corn
3 chopped onions
2 cups of chopped red and green peppers
½ cup of finely chopped hot peppers
3 cups of vinegar
2 cups of sugar
1 tbsp of salt
2 tsp of dry mustard
2 tsp of celery seed
1½ tsp of turmeric
Canning jars

Preparation:
Combine corn, onions, bell peppers, hot peppers, vinegar, sugar, salt, mustard, celery seed, and turmeric in a pot
Slowly bring it to a boil
Reduce the heat to low and simmer it for 20 minutes
Turn off the heat

Carefully fill the hot canning jars with the relish
Leave about an 1/8 inch of space at the top
Place canning lids on the jars
Tighten and turn the jars upside down so that all the heat is on the seals
Turn them back upright once the jars are completely cool
Refrigerate and begin to serve the next day
Enjoy

Sweet Chow Relish

Ingredients:
   One chopped medium cabbage head
   1 sweet onion chopped fine
   1 chopped bell pepper
   1 tbsp of salt

Preparation:
Mix the chopped vegetables and sprinkle with salt
Refrigerate for 7 hours and drain out any water
Combine the following ingredients in a large pot and simmer for 15 minutes
2 cups of vinegar
2 cups of sugar
2 tbsp of dry mustard powder
1 tsp of turmeric
1 tsp of ground ginger
2 tsp of celery seeds
Then add in the vegetables and simmer for 10 minutes
Then bring it to a boil
Spoon the vegetables into hot canning jars, covering them with the juice
Leave about an 1/8 inch of space at the top
Place canning lids on the jars
Tighten and turn the jars upside down so that all the heat is on the seals
Turn them back upright once the jars are completely cool
Refrigerate and begin to serve the next day
Enjoy

Chow-chow
Ingredients:
- 2 chopped green tomatoes
- 1 chopped bell pepper
- 1 cup of chopped cabbage
- 1 chopped medium cucumber
- 2 chopped onions
- 4 pints of water
- 2 tbsp of salt
- 2 chopped carrots
- 1 cup of chopped green beans
- 3 tsp of mustard seed
- 2 tsp of celery seed
- 2½ cups of vinegar
- 2 cups of sugar

Preparation:
Salt and soak the tomatoes, peppers, cucumber and onions overnight in water
Drain
Separately cook the carrots and green beans for 12 minutes and drain
Then mix all the ingredients in a pot
Bring it to a boil
Then spoon the vegetables into hot canning jars, covering them with the juice
Leave about an 1/8 inch of space at the top
Place canning lids on jars
Tighten and turn the jars upside down so that all the heat is on the seals
Turn them back upright once the jars are completely cool
Refrigerate and begin to serve the next day
Enjoy

Cucumber slices (Bread and butter)

Ingredients:
- 12 cups of sliced cucumbers
- 1 cup of sliced onion
- 6 cups of vinegar
- 3 cups of sugar
- 1 gallon of water
- 6 tbsp of Allspice seasoning

Preparation:
Add the water, sugar and vinegar to a pot
Add the cucumber slices, onion slices and allspice seasoning
Allow it to boil at high continuously for 25 minutes
The cucumber slices should be firm and tender
Scoop the cucumber and liquid into canning jars
Boil water in another pot that is half full
Secure the lids on the filled jars
Place the closed jars in the pot of boiling water and allow them to boil for 20 minutes
This will seal the jars and preserve the cucumber slices
Remove them with canning tongs and set them out to cool for about 12 hours
They will remain airtight and preserved until opened
Enjoy

Other

Sugar
Honey or Molasses

Stevia
The stevia plant leaves dried, ground and used as a sweetener

From sugar beets
Scrub the sugar beets well and chop them up into small pieces
Cover the beet pieces with water in a large pot and bring to a boil

Cook them until they are tender and the juice is boiled out of
the beets
Drain out the juice and reserve it
Then boil down the juice to a 1/3 of its original amount
Let it cool and it will form crystals
Scrape out the crystals and set them aside
Repeat the process with the remaining juice
Scrape out the crystals and set them aside
Keep doing this until all the juice is gone
The crystals may be used as sugar
They will not be pure white and may have a slight beet flavour
Store it in a jar tightly closed with a lid
Enjoy

Meadowsweet
Flowers have a sweet taste and may be used as sugar (may
be dried and ground)

Vinegar
Vinegar can be made from apples (cider vinegar), grapes
(wine vinegar), berries, or other fruits
Sweet apples and grapes make strong vinegar
Sour apples have a high fruit acid content and this is also
good

Apple cider vinegar
Allow sweet cider to stand in an open jug up to 6 weeks to
turn to vinegar

Mother of vinegar - recipe
Mix the amount of one-half vinegar and one-half cider
Leave it open at a temperature of 80° F for a few days
A thin scum will form on the surface and is called - mother
of vinegar
It as a vinegar starter when added to fresh apple cider pro-
duces more vinegar

Sweet apple cider
Wash and slice fully ripened apples, free of decay or bad spots
Press out the juice with a cider press or juice press
Boil the juice in a stainless steel or enamel pot until it reduces by one-half
Keep skimming it
Pour it into bottles or a stone jug and cork
Enjoy

Cooking oil
Peanuts, other nuts or sunflower seeds may be used
Roast the nuts or seeds (do not burn them)
Then grind them into a paste
Then boil the paste in water
The oil that rises to the surface may then be skimmed off and used
Otherwise use a decanter
The oil floating on top of the water may be separated with a separation funnel
It has a stopcock at the bottom allowing you to pour out the water under the oil
Enjoy

Corn oil
The wet or dry corn kernels may be ground into a paste
Then the paste should be boiled in water for about 10 minutes
Oil that rises to the surface may then be skimmed off and used
Otherwise use a decanter
The oil floating on top of the water may be separated with a separation funnel
It has a stopcock at the bottom allowing you to pour out the water under the oil
Enjoy

Olive oil

Pressed
Separate the olives from any leaves and twigs
Wash the olives in water
Dry the wet olives (spin dry or pat dry)
Then cut off and separate the olive flesh from the kernels
Crush the olive flesh into a fine paste (Millstones or heavy rocks may be used)
Slowly churn the paste for 1 hour for larger olive drops to form
(The oil and water suspension will break down and release droplets of oil)
Then press out the oil from the paste

You may do so by placing the paste between disks stacked on top of each other
One method is to stack fibre disks on top of each other in an olive press
Put pressure on the disks
As the olive paste is compacted, the liquid is pressed out
Remove the disks and the solids
Place the liquid in a jar
The water and oil will separate
Oil that rises to the surface may then be poured off and used as olive oil
Otherwise use a decanter
The oil floating on top of the water may be separated with a separation funnel
It has a stopcock at the bottom allowing you to pour out the water under the oil
Then bottle the oil
Keep the oil in a cool, dark place and enjoy (It may last several years)

How to make truffle oil
Ingredients:
One truffle – the size of a walnut, chopped into small pieces
16 oz of cooking oil
Preparation:
Add the truffle pieces to the oil
Bottle and store the truffle oil in a cool, dark place
Fill each bottle completely and keep it tightly closed
Place sealing wax over the bottle top to keep the oxygen out
Allow to sit for several weeks
Enjoy

Wine:
Pure grape wine
Squeeze out 1 gal of grape juice from good ripe grapes
Mix with 3 lbs of sugar in a container
Cover with a cloth and allow it to ferment
Get ready to bottle
Sanitize the bottles
Soak the corks of the bottles in water for about 3 hours until soft
Fill the bottles
Leave enough room under the cork for the compressed air to sit
Press the corks in the bottles (One may use a hand corker)
Waiting for the wine to mature takes patience
Lay bottles in a dark place on their side to keep the corks wet
Turn them from time to time
It needs to age
Enjoy

Chickweed wine
Ingredients:
> 5 cups of chickweed
> 3 lbs of sugar
> 2 oranges
> 1 tsp of nutrient yeast
> 1 gallon of water

Preparation:
Boil 1 gallon of water
Wash the chickweed
Peel the oranges
Remove the white pith of the peels
Add the peels to the chickweed
Pour boiling water over them
Allow them to cool
Strain the liquid and discard the chickweed and peelings
Add the sugar, stir and dissolve it
Stir in the juice of the oranges
Add the remaining ingredients and cover it with a clean cloth
Ferment it for 8 days and then siphon off the clear liquid into an airtight container
Continue to do this every 30 days
Do this until the wine is clear and no further sediments are dropped
Sweeten if it needs to be sweetened
Get ready to bottle
Sanitize the bottles
Soak the corks in water for about 3 hours until soft
Fill the bottles
Leave enough room under the cork for the compressed air to sit
Press the corks in the bottles (One may use a hand corker)
Waiting for the wine to mature takes patience
Lay bottles in a dark place on their side to keep the corks wet
Turn them from time to time
It needs to be aged at least two years
Enjoy

Elderberry wine
Ingredients:
    3½ lbs of fresh, ripe, de-stemmed elderberries
    2¼ lbs of sugar
    3½ quarts of water
    2 tsp of acid blend
    1 tsp of yeast nutrient
    ½ tsp of pectic enzyme
    1 crushed Campden tablet

Preparation:
Bring the water to boil in a pot and stir in the sugar until it is dissolved
Tie the elderberries in a straining bag (possibly a stocking)
Use sterilized rubber gloves and mash the elderberries in the bag
Cover the bag with the sugar-water and set aside to cool
When it is lukewarm, add the acid blend, yeast nutrient and crushed Campden tablet
Cover and wait 15 hours and then stir in the pectic enzyme
Stir it daily
Again using sterilized gloves gently squeeze the bag to extract the berry flavour
Ferment it for 15 days
Remove the bag
Siphon the wine into narrow neck bottles
Fill to a ¼ inch below an air stopper
Keep it attached to prevent air and oxidation
Put in a dark place and ferment for 70 days
Repeat this process for 70 days
Repeat the process again for 70 days
Now siphon and sweeten to taste
Sanitize the bottles
Soak the corks in water for about 3 hours until soft
Fill the bottles
Leave enough room under the cork for the compressed air to sit
Press the corks in the bottles (One may use a hand corker)
Waiting for the wine to mature takes patience
Lay bottles in a dark place on their side to keep the corks wet
Turn them from time to time
Enjoy

Dandelion wine
Ingredients:
   3 quarts of fresh dandelion flowers
   1 lb of raisins
   1 gallon of water
   3 lbs granulated sugar

3 oranges
1 tsp of yeast nutrient

Preparation:
Pick the petals off the flowers and put in a bowl
Boil 9 pints of water
Set aside 1 pint of water
Pour the boiling water over the dandelion flowers and cover tightly
Leave for two days, stirring daily
Pour the mixture into a pot and bring it to a boil
Add the sugar
Remove the white pith of the orange peels
Add the oranges
Boil for 80 minutes and pour into a container
Now add the juice and pulp of the oranges
Allow to cool to 70° F
Add the yeast nutrient
Cover it and put it in a warm place for four days
Strain and pour into a fermentation container
Add the raisins and fit on an airlock
After the wine clears, strain it
Leave until the fermentation ceases completely
Siphon into a container and set aside for 3 months
Sanitize the bottles
Soak the corks in water for about 3 hours until soft
Fill the bottles
Leave enough room under the cork for the compressed air to sit
Wine must age at least 10 months
Lay bottles in a dark place on their side to keep the corks wet
Turn them from time to time
Enjoy

Pawpaw wine
Ingredients:
    4 lbs of ripe paw paws peeled and cut into pieces
    3 lbs of sugar
    8 pts of water
    1½ tsp of citric acid

1 tsp of pectic enzyme
½ tsp of grape tannin
1 tsp of yeast nutrient

Preparation:
Boil the water
Tie the fruit in a straining bag (Possibly a stocking)
Mash the fruit in the bag, place it in a container and pour sugar over it
Pour the boiling water over it
Cover and set it aside to cool
When it reaches room temperature, add all other ingredients (except yeast)
Now set aside for 15 hours
Then add the yeast
When it ferments stir it three times per day for 8 days
Squeeze most of the juice out of the bag
Pour it into another container and fit on an airlock
Set aside for 3 months
Siphon the cleared liquid into a sterilized container and refit the airlock
After 3 months repeat this again
Once the wine has cleared it is time for bottling
Sanitize the bottles
Soak the corks in water for about 3 hours until soft
Fill the bottles
Leave enough room under the cork for the compressed air to sit
Press the corks in the bottles (One may use a hand corker)
Wine must age at least 10 months
Lay bottles in a dark place on their side to keep the corks wet
Turn them from time to time and enjoy

Condiment and flavour substitutes:

Mint –
- Bergamot flowering tops
Lemon –
- Sorrel leaves and flowers
Curry –
- Perilla plant leaves
Mustard
- Charlock ground seeds
- Winter cress ground seeds
- Mustard ground seeds
Ginger
- Shepherd's Purse root
- Sweet flag root
Cloves
– Water Aven root
Pepper
- Pepper grass seeds (October)
- Goldenrod flowers
- Wild pepper
Salt
- Solomon Seal roots
Sugar
- Sugar beets (see recipe)
- Honey
- Molasses
Cumin
- Pignut tubers
Garlic
- Ramps
Aniseed
- Sweet Cicely leaves
Vanilla
- Sweet clover blossoms - dried
Root beer flavour
- Sassafras leaves

Living in Difficult Times

Special recognition and acknowledgements:

My book has a general approach on how to live in difficult times
It is very limited and I encourage readers to obtain more information, from others who are specialists in their specific fields of interest.

There are numerous excellent wild plant foraging experts, who have published and produced the following:
Books
DVD's
Videos
Training material
Recipes

Here are some of the websites I have visited:

http://www.altnature.com/Herbs2003/index.html
https://ofthefield.com/resources/products_detail.php?ProductID=2
http://www.learningherbs.com/wild_edible_plant_cards.html
http://www.herbvideos.com/
http://www.wildmanstevebrill.com
http://www.theforagerpress.com/fieldguide/recipes/recipes.htm
http://www.food.yahoo.com/recipes
http://www.wildliferecipes.net/index.asp
http://www.learningherbs.com/dandelion_recipes.html
http://www.southernfood.about.com/cs/ramps/a/ramps.htm
http://www.writerbynature.com/category/wild-food-recipes/
http://www.wildmanwildfood.co.uk/pages/recipes.htm
http://www.natureskills.com/wild_food_recipe.html
http://www.prodigalgardens.info/
http://www.native-american-online.org/food.htm
http://www.wildfoods.info/index.html
http://www.grandpappy.info/rkudzu.htm
http://www.crabappleherbs.com/blog/category/food/recipes/

http://www.wildpantry.com/recipes.htm
http://www.finestchef.com/wild_game_recipes.htm

You may also choose to do an online **search** for information you require on **edible** or **medicinal** wild plants and recipes. I have enjoyed receiving a wealth of information by going online to YouTube at
www.youtube.com

Books I have enjoyed reading:
- Edible Wild Mushrooms of North America by David W Fisher
- The Gathering Place – by Johnnie Sue Myers (Traditional Cherokee dishes)

Wild Cards that that I have found extremely useful - I highly recommend this!
These are a regular deck of playing cards with 52 common wild edible food plants.
One side of the card has a colour photo, line drawing and a RANGE MAP for the plant.
The other side tells you what part of the plant is edible, what the uses are, characteristics of the plant and REALLY HELPFUL hints about that plant.
It also includes the botanical name and other common names.
It may be purchased from - http://www.learningherbs.com/wild_edible_plant_cards.html

Notes
Additional recipes

Chapter Eight:
Making your own cosmetics and home products

The author has acquired many useful cosmetic and home product recipes.

He has applied or modified various selections for improved satisfaction and success.

Many of the recipes -
- Have been passed down from grandparents to their children and grandchildren.
- Are from indigenous tribal Indians or individuals.
- Have been passed down to descendants of early settlers and pioneers.

Disclaimer:

The recipes, methods and information presented herein are intended for your reading pleasure. Experiencing success and enjoyment of the recipes may vary from person to person. The writer and publisher make no warranties, expressed or implied, regarding the success, satisfaction and accuracy of the recipes provided. The writer and publisher, also assume no legal or other liability and responsibility, for any loss or injuries that may result from using the recipes or information. However every effort has been made to avoid errors, omissions and outdated or incorrect information.

In order to achieve success with the recipes, users may need to adjust the quantities or change the ingredients according to their own taste and satisfaction.

Using the recipes and information in this book will constitute your acceptance of this disclaimer.

Measuring – tsp = teaspoon - tbsp = tablespoon

Moisturizing Cream
Boil 3 cups of water and pour it over the Herbs of your choice
Simmer it for 20 minutes, strain it and set the liquid aside to cool
Combine a mixture of 2/3 of a cup of any combination of oils, such as -
(Rosehip oil, Camellia oil, Evening Primrose oil, Sunflower oil or Vitamin E oil)
Then
Microwave ¼ cup of soy wax in a glass bowl on high for about 3 minutes, until melted
Mix in the oil mixture
Add it in a steady stream to the herb water while beating until creamy and smooth
Allow the cream to cool and spoon into a jar
Close the jar and store in a cool place
Use

Body lotion
Ingredients:
   1 cup of Lanolin
   ½ cup of Shea Butter
   ¼ cup of Jojoba Oil
   5 tbsp of Vitamin E Acetate
   ½ cup of Liquid Glycerine

Preparation:
Heat and stir all the ingredients until melted
Cool and pour into a container
Store in cool place and use

Hand cream
   Take 1 lb of pure beeswax and melt it
   Take 3 lbs in weight of olive oil

Place both in a double boiler or a glass bowl over a pan of simmering water, to melt
Gently mix in any additives or petals of your choice -
(A few drops of lavender or geranium essential oil, aloe vera or calendula)
(Petals – like Rose, chamomile or dried marigold)
Gently warm again and strain
Allow the cream to cool and pour into a jar
Store in cool place and use

Toothpaste
Use baking soda mixed with a flavour
(Spearmint, Peppermint, Anise, Fennel, Cinnamon)
or
Place 4 tsp of baking soda in a jar
Mix in water till it forms a paste
Add 8 drops of peroxide
Flavour it according to choice (Spearmint, Peppermint, Anise, Fennel or Cinnamon)
Mix in 1 cup of glycerine
Spoon into a container and close
Use the paste to brush your teeth

Shampoo - **for normal hair**
Place 4 cups of a herb blend in 4 cups of boiling water
(Chamomile, Nettle, Sage, Rosemary or other)
Steep for 15 minutes and strain
Add 4 cups of chopped soap of your choice
Boil at low in a covered stainless steel pot until the soap has dissolved
Remove from heat and allow it to cool
Add a fragrance, pour into a container and close with a lid
Store in a cool place and use as a shampoo

Shampoo - **for dry hair**
Place 4 cups of a herb blend in 4 cups of boiling water
(Chamomile, Nettle, Sage, Rosemary or other)
Steep for 15 minutes and strain

Add 4 cups of chopped soap of your choice
Boil on low in a covered stainless steel pot until the soap has dissolved
Remove from heat and allow it to cool
Mix in ¼ cup of olive oil
Add a fragrance, pour into a container and close with a lid
Store in a cool place and use as a shampoo

Cologne or perfume
Boil containers in water to ensure that they are as sterile and allow to dry
Always store essential oils and fragrances in a cool dry place
Never use metal instruments
If glycerine is blended with water, always prevent air bubbles
Equipment:
Measuring cups
Measuring spoons
A narrow funnel
A small glass pitcher
Glass bottles
Droppers
A grinding mill (manual or electric)

Ingredients:
2 cups of a flower blend of your choice ground in a mill (Any flowers)
2 cups of water
2 cups of alcohol (like vodka)
6 tsp of essential oils (lemon, bergamot, rosemary, jasmine or other)
2 tsp of glycerine

Preparation:
Place 2 cups of the flower blend in 2 cups of boiling water
Steep for 15 minutes and strain
Place a piece of orange peel at the bottom of a glass container
Blend the fragrant water with the glycerine and add to the glass container

Add the alcohol and then the essential oils
Cap the glass container tightly and place in a cool, dark place for 5 weeks
Filter and pour the mixture into cologne or perfume bottles
Package and store in cool place
Use

Body soap
Ingredients:
36 oz of the oil of your choice
Possibly a combination of the following -
    14 oz of Olive Oil
    10 oz of Coconut Oil
    10 oz of Palm Oil
    12 oz water
    4½ oz of lye solution
    ½ cup of rose petals
    2 oz of almond oil

Preparation:
Boil the water and pour it over the rose petals
Steep for 15 minutes, strain and set the liquid aside to cool
Mix in the oils
Mix in the lye solution
Pour into moulds and allow setting
Use

Laundry soap
Mix in 2 tbsp of any of the following with a cup of boiling water
(Lavender, lemon peel, orange peel, ground cloves, oregano, pine, rosemary)
Let it steep for 15 minutes and strain
Add 1 tbsp of Baking soda
Mix in 2 tbsp of Borax
(Use ½ cup of Borax if washing whites)
Use

Living in Difficult Times

Oven Cleaner
    Ingredients:
    1 cup of ammonia
    1 cup of baking soda
    ½ cup of white vinegar

Preparation:
Preheat the oven to low
Then turn off the heat
Put the ammonia in a pan in the closed oven for 5 hours
Remove
Mix the vinegar and soda in a jar
Use this as a paste to scrub the sides of the oven
Then fine spray the oven with water and wipe it clean

Glass cleaner
    1 cup of vinegar
    1 cup of alcohol (Vodka)
    1 cup of water

Peparation:
Combine in a spray bottle
Use on windows, mirrors, appliances and faucets

Laundry washing soap
    1 bar of soap cut into pieces
    Add to 2 litres of hot water
    Boil and stir to melt
    Add 1 cup of Borax
    Add 1 cup of baking soda
    Boil and mix
    Pour into a 2 gal jar
    Fill with hot water
    Let sit for 30 hours
    Use ½ cup per washing load

Chapter Eight: Making your own cosmetics and home products

Deodorant **(Spray)**

Ingredients:
- ½ cup of witch hazel
- ½ cup of aloe-vera juice
- ½ cup of distilled water
- 30 drops of the oil of your choice (rosemary, tea tree, lavender)
- 2 tsp of glycerine

Preparation:
Mix together all the ingredients
Pour into a spray bottle
When using – shake it well and spray where needed
Store in a cool location

Deodorant **(Powder)**

Mix 1½ oz of baking soda with 8 oz of cornstarch in a container with a lid
Mix and shake it well
Apply to the skin or under your armpits

Deodorant **(Stick)**

Ingredients:
- ½ cup of Baking soda
- ½ cup of Corn Starch
- 30 drops of the oil of your choice (rosemary, tea tree, lavender)
- An empty Deodorant container (new or used)
- 7 tbsp of Shortening at room temperature

Preparation:
Mix ½ cup of baking soda and ½ cup of cornstarch in a bowl
Add 30 drops of the oil of your choice
Stir in 7 tbsp of shortening (lard) to the consistency of a paste
Press the mixture into a deodorant container
Allow to set to become firm
Apply to the skin or under your armpits

Living in Difficult Times

After shave
   Ingredients:
   6 tbsp of witch hazel
   9 tbsp of cider vinegar
   15 tbsp of flower water
   (Orange peels or other flowers steeped in boiling water for 20 minutes)
   30 drops of any essential oil
   (Orange, Sandalwood, Bergamot, Lavender or other)

Preparation:
Combine all the ingredients into a bottle and shake well
Set it aside for 8 days
Shake it before using
Store in a cool dark place and use

Cologne
Ingredients:
   ½ cup of distilled water
   ½ cup of alcohol (or vodka)
   20 drops of essential oil
   (Orange peels, Lemon, Sandalwood, Bergamot, Lavender or other)

Preparation:
Mix in the essential oils and alcohol in a bottle and shake well
Set aside for 30 days
Add the distilled water then set aside for 10 days
Shake it before using
Store in a cool dark place and use

Black shoe polish
(Never prepare this recipe near a lighted stove or naked flame)
Melt 10 oz of bees wax in a container that is placed in another container of water
(The bees wax should fill less than ½ of the container)
Bring the water to a boil
Stir in 1 oz of potash (potassium carbonate)

The mixture will foam up (be careful to avoid the danger of burning)
Then set it aside
Dissolve 5 cups of black charcoal powder in a little cold water
Add it to the bees wax
Bring it to a boil and then simmer it for 5 minutes, stirring it until it creams
Remove from the heat and stir in some turpentine for a creamy constituency
Add to a container or used polish tin that can close tightly

Brown shoe polish
(Never prepare this recipe near a lighted stove or naked flame)
Melt 10 oz of bees wax in a container that is placed in another container of water
(The bees wax should fill less than ½ of the container)
Bring the water to a boil
Stir in 1 oz of potash (potassium carbonate)
The mixture will foam up (be careful to avoid the danger of burning)
Then set it aside
Add black walnut dye (as needed) to the bees wax water (see recipe below)
Bring it to a boil and then simmer it for 5 minutes, stirring it until it creams
Remove from the heat and stir in some turpentine to a creamy constituency
Add to a container or used polish tin that can close tightly
Instead of the black walnut dye one may also use finely ground instant coffee

Walnut dye
Gather black walnuts from the ground
You can find them on the ground under a walnut tree during the fall
Cut the hulls away from the nuts
Use the hulls - discard the nuts for another purpose
Create the dye by placing the hulls in a nylon stocking
Soak them in a pot of water overnight

Squeeze the dye out of the stocking to obtain a dark brown colour
This will keep the hulls out of the dye
Then boil the water to use as a dye
Add a small amount of white vinegar to the dye to prevent it from moulding
Use the dye as needed
(It may be poured into containers and frozen for later use)

Generally needed ingredients to make many of the above products:

Lanolin
Shea Butter
Colourless Jojoba Oil
Vitamin E Acetate
Liquid Glycerine
Olive Oil
Coconut Oil
Palm Oil
Lye
Sweet Almond Oil
Flower Petals
Beeswax
Lavender essential oil
Lemon essential oil
Orange Lemon essential oil
Baking soda
Peroxide
Glycerine
Alcohol
Borax

These basic ingredients may be purchased from any of the following:
http://www.allnaturalcosmetics4u.com/rawingredients
http://www.essentialwholesale.com/
http://www.makingcosmetics.com/

http://www.naturalcosmeticsupplies.com/perfume-fra-grance-ingredients.html
One may also Google search for other suppliers

Natural Colour dyes:
The following will render different colours -
Yellow
Goldenrod, orange or lemon peels, celery seed, ground cumin or ground turmeric
Green
Chlorophyll from spinach or greens
Pink/red
Pomegranate juice, red onion skins, beet juice or red cabbage juice
Pink
Strawberries, pink roses, chopped rhubarb stalks, cranberry juice, raspberries or red grapes
Red
Bloodroot
Orange
Yellow onion skins or paprika
Dark orange
Chilli powder
Greenish yellow
Yellow delicious apple peels
Blue
Blueberry juice, blackberries or purple grapes
Lavender
Mixture of purple grape juice, violet blossoms, two tsp of lemon juice, red onion skin juice
Brown
Dill seeds, black walnut shells or instant coffee
Purple
Mulberries, cedar root or red maple
Black
Charcoal
Gold
Barberry root

Notes
Additional recipes

Chapter Nine:
Information about wild plants and remedies, used for wellness

Read this disclaimer

Information presented herein is for your reading pleasure and research purposes only.

The Author and Publisher is not a botanist or licensed health-care professional.

He makes no warranties, expressed or implied, regarding the accuracy or efficacy of the information provided in this book.

It is not his intention to advise on health issues.

Please see a medical professional about any health concerns you have.

The information and statements in this book have not been evaluated by the FDA.

The information in this book is not intended to prevent, diagnose, treat, or cure any disease.

If any of the information is applied, individual results or reactions may vary from person to person.

Therefore before using any of the information provided herein, it is always advisable to consult with your Doctor or Healthcare Provider first.

When undergoing any medical treatment or procedures, readers or those they are advising, should consult their medical practitioners before making decisions about their medical prescriptions and treatments.

Those who are experiencing allergies should consult their medical practitioners before making decisions about any medical prescriptions and treatments.

It is also advisable for readers to do farther research. They may do so from other sources, comparing and substantiating all the information before applying it.

It is also advisable to always use a small amount of the doses indicated first, to ensure that there are no allergic or negative reactions.

It is important to be able to correctly identify wild plants and ingredients before usage.

There are lookalike plants that are poisonous such as Poison Hemlock, Jimson weed, and others.

If using herbs always do so responsibly and know what you are doing, so as to safeguard yourself.

If herbs are used in excessive amounts or combined with pre-scription drugs or alcohol, they can be harmful.

Reading and using information in this book will consti-tute your acceptance of this disclaimer.

Throughout the ages, people have discovered the usefulness of wild plants and remedies for wellness and sickness.

There are many wild plants in nature that have great medici-nal value.

Again, one must be careful when foraging to avoid harmful lookalikes.

Be sure to consult with a knowledgeable person if unsure or in doubt when identifying any plant.

There are many natural foods, substances and recipes that are helpful in treating ailments and sicknesses.

Notes
Additional information about
medicinal wild plants

The following preparations may be used in preparing ingredients:
Plants, leaves, flowers or roots should always be thoroughly cleaned before being used as a paste, poultice, infusion, tea, tincture or decoction.

A Paste
Plants, roots or materials ground into a paste, may be applied to the affected area.

A Poultice
It is a warm moist preparation of ground roots or crushed leaves, placed on an aching or inflamed part of the body easing pain and bringing relief.

An Infusion
Oil infusion
Made of cut of roots or crushed leaves that are placed in oil for a time and strained for use.
The liquid is rubbed on or applied where needed.

A cold water infusion
Made by placing cut roots or crushed leaves in water for a time and strained to use as a rub or drink as indicated.

A Tea
Made by placing cut roots or crushed leaves in hot or cold water for a time and strained to drink.

A Tincture
Made of cut roots or crushed leaves placed in alcohol for a time and strained to use.
It is used for internal or external use as indicated.

A Decoction
Made by boiling the stem, twig, flower, leaf or bud of a plant for as long as indicated and then used as indicated.

Dosage – generally used
Adult dosage (age 17 and older)
When using crushed or ground dried roots and leaves, one teaspoon is generally used in one cup of water or liquid or as otherwise indicated.
When using fresh crushed or ground roots and leaves, 3 teaspoons are generally used in one cup of water or liquid or as otherwise indicated.

Child dosage (Age 9-16)
Half those of adults

Children under 8 years of age should not be given any dosage

Here is information for ailments in alphabetical order:

Acne
Acne skin
Mix and simmer 1 finely diced dandelion, 1 tbsp of honey and 1 tbsp of ground sarsaparilla vine root in water. Allow to sit for 15 minutes, strain and drink
or
Acne skin that is oily
Apply egg white as a mask to the affected area
Allow the mask to dry
Leave it for 10 minutes and wash it off
Then apply pure aloe-vera juice on the skin, leave for 10 minutes and wash off

Alcoholism
Kudzu root tea - 4 teaspoons of fresh cut kudzu root, simmered in 1 litre of boiling water for 15 minutes and strain (Use 3 times per day - up to 8 weeks)
This will make drinking alcohol unpleasant

Allergies
Of the nasal cavity
Mix a ½ tsp of baking soda in 1 cup of lukewarm water
Spray or squirt it into each nostril
Wipe away unwanted mucous that comes out
Of the skin
Possible causes -
- Oily Skin
- Impure blood
- Gluten allergy
- Other allergies caused by -
Metals like Gold or Nickel in jewellery and clasps or buttons on clothing
Antibiotics in creams, ointments, cosmetics, deodorants, soap, and pet food
Fragrances in foods, cosmetics, insecticides, antiseptics, soaps, perfumes, and products
Preservatives in antiseptics
Preservatives in paper, paints, medications, cleaners, cosmetics and fabrics
Preservatives in cosmetic products, self-tanners, shampoo, nail polish and sunscreen Preservatives in industrial products such as polishes, paints, and waxes
Treatments -
Apply sage oil once per day to allergic areas
Include beetroot in the diet
Face masks for an oily skin
Blood cleansers
Avoid the substance to which you are allergic
Use a corticosteroid cream

Anaemia
Add Alfalfa Herb leaves to your diet
(Do not use if you are taking a blood thinning agent)
Add dark green leafy vegetables to your diet

Chapter Nine: Information about wild plants and remedies

Asthma
Eat Bee pollen
Tea of 2 tsp of Sumac leaves steeped in 1 cup of boiling water for 2 minutes
Tea of 2 tsp of Myrrh gum bark steeped in 1 cup of boiling water for 10 minutes
Tea of 2 tsp of Mullein leaf steeped in 1 cup of boiling water for 10 minutes
Tea of 2 tsp of Pleurisy root steeped in 1 cup of boiling water for 10 minutes
Tea of 2 tsp of cut Indian turnip root steeped in 1 cup of boiling water for 10 minutes
Tea of 2 tsp of ground Goldenseal roots steeped in boiling water for 10 minutes
(2 cups per day)
6 grams of powdered Black Cohosh root simmered as a tea in 1 cup of water
Use 1 tsp, 3 times a day (for no longer than 4 months)
Lobelia herb dried leaves smoked as tobacco to inhale the smoke
Eat Capsicum fruit

Antibacterial
Bayberry Root Bark crushed into a paste and applied to the external bacterial area
(Do not take during Pregnancy)

Antibiotics
Garlic cloves chopped and eaten raw, or on bread or mixed in food
Goldenseal root tea - 3 tsp of raw cut root steeped in a cup of boiling water for 10 minutes (2 cups per day)
Red Root tea - 3 tsp of raw cut root per cup, steeped in boiling water for 10 minutes (2 cups per day)
Blue violet leaves in a salad
1 oz of dried Heal all herb steeped in 1 pint of boiling water for 10 minutes and sweetened with honey

Antioxidants are helpful
When molecules in the body oxidize, they create free-radicals. Excessive free radicals wreak havoc on our cellular structures. They cause the molecules within the cells to become unstable. It is said that they have a "chain-reaction" effect in the formation of cancerous cells.
That is why we need antioxidants.
Antioxidants find their way into the body, mostly through the foods we eat.
They slow down and prevent molecules to oxidate.

Numerous antioxidants:
Vitamin C
Vitamin E
Coenzyme Q 10
Lipoic acid
Glutathione
Grape nuts

Antiseptic
Red oak bark ground into a paste and applied to the external bacterial area
Barberry Root (Yellow Root) ground and mixed in a cream and applied to the infected area (Do not take during Pregnancy)

Anxiety disorders
Tea made of 1 Passion fruit flower steeped in a cup of boiling water for 10 minutes
Magnesium – derived from fish, nuts, dried apricots and whole grains

Appetite builder
Tea made of 1 Dandelion flower steeped in 1 cup of boiling water for 10 minutes

Chapter Nine: Information about wild plants and remedies

Arteries
Spinach – contains vitamin K that is said to remove calcification in arteries
Tea made of 1 tsp of dried Hawthorne leaves steeped in 1 cup of boiling water for 10 minutes (Use for cholesterol, plaque build-up, arterial damage and angina)

Arthritis
Eating 6 cherries per day
Prickly pear fruit
Pineapple that contains Bromelain
Tea made of 1 tsp of fresh Agrimony Herb steeped in 1 cup of boiling water for 10 minutes (2 cups per day)
1 tsp Alfalfa Herb steeped in 1 cup of boiling water for 10 minutes (2 cups per day)
(Don't use if you are taking a blood thinner)
Boswelia cream - applied to the affected area

Athlete's foot
Add 6 garlic cloves to a cup of olive oil and keep in a cool area for a week
Apply everyday to the affected area

Bee sting
Remove the stinger gently scraping it off with a butter knife or credit card
(Don't squeeze)
Apply tobacco juice to the sting – it helps to draw it out

Bleeding
External:
Stop the bleeding by applying direct pressure on the supplying artery, slowing the flow of blood to the injured area
A wound may be filled with cayenne pepper to help stop bleeding and bring healing
Shepherds purse leaves may be applied to the external bleeding area
Agrimony herb leaves may be applied to the external bleeding area

White vinegar stops most bleeding on contact and may be applied to the external bleeding area

A wad of spider web may be applied to a small external bleeding area

(Dirt and the spider must first be removed from the web before using)

Internal:

Drink 3 teaspoons of crushed Mullein in a glass of milk

Tea made of 3 tsp of fresh Shepherds purse leaves per cup, steeped in boiling water for 10 minutes (drink one-half cup every hour)

Blood circulation stimulation and inhibiting blood clots

Pure grape juice

(Not to be used during pregnancy or by persons taking blood thinning agents)

Place 1 tsp of cut Ginkgo Biloba roots in 1 cup of water for 12 hours, strain and drink the liquid

Tea made of 1 tsp of fresh Hyssop herb leaves per cup, steeped in boiling water for 10 minutes

Tea made of 1 tsp of fresh Sweet Birch leaves per cup, steeped in boiling water for 10 minutes (It has aspirin ingredients)

Willow tree – scrape the thin layer under the bark and use ½ tsp (It has aspirin ingredients)

Tea made of 1 tsp of Angelica Root in 1 cup of boiling water, simmered for 5 minutes

(3 cups per day)

Blood builder

Tea made of 3 tsp of fresh Sassafras leaves or cut roots per cup, steeped in boiling water for 10 minutes

Tea made of 3 tsp of fresh Wild strawberry leaves per cup, steeped in boiling water for 10 minutes

Blood pressure

Reduce sodium (avoid salt) intake and increase potassium intake (eat a banana)

Garlic cloves eaten raw or mixed in food

Tea made of one Passion flower steeped in 1 cup boiling water for 10 minutes

3 tsp of Rue herb steeped in 1 cup of boiling water for 10 minutes

Blood cleanser
Onions – eaten raw
Ginger – used in food and drinks
Place 3 tsp of Ginkgo Biloba cut roots in water for 12 hours, strain and drink
Place young tender cut Pokeweed leaves (April) in water for 12 hours, strain and drink
A tea made of 3 tsp of cut Burdock leaves steeped in 1 cup of boiling water for 10 minutes
A tea made of 3 tsp of the Sugar Maple inner bark, steeped in 1 cup of boiling water for 10 minutes

Blood sugar – to lower blood sugar levels
Place 1 tsp of cut Alisma roots in 1 cup of water for 12 hours, strain and drink
Place 1 tsp of cut Devil's Club Root Bark in 1 cup of water for 12 hours, strain and drink
Drink a tea of 4 teaspoons of fresh kudzu root, simmered in 1 litre of boiling water for 15 minutes (Use 3 times per day - up to 8 weeks)

Blood thinning
Garlic cloves eaten raw

Body builder – natural steroids
Place 3 tsp of cut Trillium root in 1 cup of water for 12 hours, strain and drink 1 tbsp per day
Place 3 tsp of cut Wild yam root roots in 1 cup of water for 10 hours, strain and drink 1 tbsp per day
Place 3 tsp of cut Yellow dock root in 1 cup of water for 12 hours, strain and drink 1 tbsp per day
Place 1 tsp of cut Yucca root in 1 cup of water for 12 hours, strain and drink 1 tbsp per day

Boils
Jack in pulpit roots ground and made into a poultice and applied to the boil

Bones – to strengthen
Calcium
Celery

Bowel that is weak
Drink a tea made of 1 tsp of crushed White oak bark, steeped in 1 cup of boiling water for 10 minutes

Burns
Apply mustard to the burn
Fresh cut potatoes applied to the burn area – for instant soothing relief
Apply washed, clean, crushed cattail roots to the burn for soothing relief

Cancer
External
Sheep sorrel leaves poultice (fresh) applied to the external cancer
Wood sorrel plant poultice (fresh) applied to the external cancer
Plantain leaf poultice (fresh) applied to the external cancer
Poke berries poultice (fresh) applied to the external cancer
Solomon seal root poultice (fresh) applied to the skin cancer
Iron weed leaves or root poultice (fresh) applied to the tumour
Internal
Vitamin D
Tarragon tea
Broccoli sprouts
Sheep sorrel leaves
One Pawpaw (Asimina Tribola) fruit eaten 3 times per day (not papaya)
Place 1 tsp of cut Beech Drop roots in 1 cup of water for 12 hours, strain and drink
Tea made of 1 tsp of crushed Honeysuckle bark steeped in boiling water for 10 minutes
(For breast cancer)

Chicken pox
(Use a combination of St. John's Wort leaves, stem and flowers, cut burdock root, and cut liquorice root)
Place 1 cup of each in 1 gallon of boiling water, simmer for 20 minutes and strain
Add to bath water and soak the effected parts of the body for relief

Cholesterol
Tea made of 1 tsp of crushed Honeysuckle bark steeped in 1 cup of boiling water for 10 minutes
Eat lots of Fibre in your diet

Cleansing
Blood
Three days fasting – no food just water
or
Drink a tea made by boiling 2 tsp of yellow dock root in 16 oz of water
or
Eat raw Onions
or
½ tsp of raw Ginger root each day for 7 days
Drink a tea made by boiling 2 tsp of Ginkgo Biloba leaves in 16 oz of water
Place 3 tsp of young Pokeweed leaves (April) in 1 cup of water for 12 hours, strain and drink the liquid
Drink a tea made by boiling 1 tsp of Burdock leaves in 2 cups of water
Drink a tea made of 3 tsp of the Sugar Maple inner bark, steeped in 1 cup of boiling water for 10 minutes
Arteries
Eat 1 clove of raw garlic per day – as a blood thinning agent it helps clean the arteries.
A new skin
Seven days of fasting – no food just water and take a hot bath very day
(Not in the case of skin burns)
Stomach and renewed stomach lining
Seven days fasting – no food just water

Kidneys
A tea made of 2 tbsp of watermelon seed boiled in 1 cup of water and left to cool
Urinary system
Drink a tea made by boiling 2 tsp of Golden Seal root in 2 cups of water
Gallbladder
Drink ½ cup of olive oil at 8pm
I hour later drink a mixture of 2 tsp of Epsom salt in 1 cup of warm water
Experience a bowel movement the next morning
Colon
Romaine lettuce eaten twice per week (use it as a salad)
Drink 1 cup of cranberry juice mixed with fibre per day for several days
Lungs
Stop smoking
Eat only pineapple and drink water for three days (a pineapple fast)
Drink a lot of water
Deep breathing three times each day
Exercise to enlarge your lungs breathing capacity
Eat crushed fresh Perilla seed or leaves (1 tsp per day)
Drink a tea made by boiling 2 tsp of fresh Maidenhair fern leaves and rhizomes in 16 oz of water
Drink a tea made by boiling 2 tsp of fresh Pleurisy root in 16 oz of water
(See asthma treatments)
Nasal
Mix ½ teaspoon of baking soda mixed with 1 cup of lukewarm water and squirt up the nose (then clear away the mucous that comes out)

Ears
(For children) Insert 1 drop of lukewarm baby oil – finger test to insure the temperature.
(For adults) Mix 1 tsp of lukewarm white vinegar with 1 tsp of alcohol and insert in the ear
– Finger test to insure the temperature.
Worm and Parasite cleanse

Pumpkin seeds eaten protect against parasites and worms
Drink a tea made of 1 tsp of crushed Black walnut hulls and leaves boiled in water
Eat ½ oz of ground Male fern rhizomes (also use for Tape worms)

Colds, flu and Pneumonia
Dark honey – 2 teaspoons daily
Chicken soup
Mullein -
Inhale the vapours of Mullein flowers boiled in water (for nasal congestion)
Tea made from 1 tsp of crushed Mullein leaves steeped in 1 cup of boiling water
(For coughs, hoarseness, and bronchitis)
Chickweed
Tea made from 2 tbsp of crushed chickweed leaves and flowers in 1 cup of water
(For bronchitis, pleurisy, coughs, colds, hoarseness, lungs, bronchial tubes)
Soapwort herb root
Place 1 tsp of cut Soapwort herb root in 1 cup of water for 12 hours, strain and drink
Yarrow flower
Drink a tea made by boiling 2 tsp in 1 cup of boiling water
Bayberry Root Bark
Tea made by boiling 1 tsp of cut Bayberry Root Bark in 1 cup of water
(Do Not Take During Pregnancy)
Beech Drop root
Place 1 tsp of cut Beech Drop root in 1 cup of water for 12 hours, strain and drink
Marshmallow root
Place 1 tsp of cut Marshmallow root in 1 cup of water for 12 hours, strain and drink
(For inflammation of the mouth, gastritis, peptic ulceration, colitis, bronchitis and an irritating cough)
Perilla seed or leaves crushed (1 tsp per day)
(An expectorant, emollient, antitussive, antiasthmatic, for phlegm and a mild laxative)

Living in Difficult Times

Induce sweating
Tea made from 2 tsp of crushed Catnip leaves, steeped in 1 cup of boiling water for 10 minutes
Tea made of 2 tsp of crushed Magnolia flower bud, steeped in 1 cup of boiling water for 10 minutes
Fennel seeds ground – 1 tsp
Loosening up mucous or phlegm
Place 2 tsp of cut Maidenhair fern leaves and rhizomes in 1 cup of water for 12 hours, strain and drink
Tea made of 2 tsp of cut Pleurisy root, steeped in 1 cup of boiling water for 10 minutes
Antihistamine
Tea made from 2 tbsp of crushed chickweed leaves, steeped in 1 cup of boiling water for 10 minutes (3 times per day)
Tea made from 1 tbsp of crushed Mullein leaves steeped in 1 cup of boiling water
(3 times per day)
Expectorant-
1 raw chopped onion
3 chopped raw cloves of garlic
or
Place 1 chopped onion and the 3 crushed cloves of a garlic in a bowl
Cover it with sugar for 2 hours
This will produce a syrup
Use 1 tbsp of the syrup 3 times per day for the congestion
or
Mix 1 minced onion with 1 cup of honey in a jar
Place in a double boiler, cook for 90 minutes and filter
Allow to cool to room temperature
Shelf life up to 1 month
Dosage
    - Adults - 1 tbsp 3 times per day
    - Children over 8 years - 1 teaspoon every 4 hours
(Not for children under 8 years of age)

Constipation
Eat whole grains, fruits, vegetables, brown rice, prunes and figs (high in fibre)

Sprinkle one teaspoon of ground flaxseeds or ground psyllium seeds over any meal
Eat fibre supplements

Contraceptive for women – said to have some success
1 tsp of freshly ground Queen Anne's lace plant seeds (ground just before taking)
Stir into a 1 glass of cold water and drink after intercourse

Cough Drops
Ingredients:
  1 cup of mullein leaves
  2 cups of brown sugar
  2 cups of boiling water
Preparation:
Steep leaves in boiled water for 70 minutes in a covered pot
Strain and add the brown sugar
Boil the mixture until it becomes soft like candy
Pour it about ½ inch thick onto a greased flat cookie sheet
Immediately cut it into small pieces and leave it to cool
Then break and wrap the pieces in wax paper for later use

Cough Medicine
1 tsp of coconut oil
Add 2 drops of oregano oil
Use up to four times per day
or
Drink a tea made by boiling 1 tsp of Pine needles in 8 oz of water
Drink a tea made by boiling 1 tsp of ground Redbud bark in 8 oz of water
(For whooping cough)
Drink a tea made by boiling 1 tsp of ground Thimbleweed in 8 oz of water
(For whooping cough)

Cough Syrup
(To relieve sore throat and clear congestion)
Ingredients:
1 oz of crushed fresh horehound herb leaves

2 oz of water
1 tbsp of powdered slippery elm bark
2 oz of honey
Preparation:
Mix the horehound in the water and boil it
Reduce it by up to 45%
Mix in the slippery elm and honey
Use up 1 tablespoon every three hours (Only for 2 days)
or
Boil ½ cup of lemon juice
Mix it with 5 tbsp of honey
Use 1 teaspoonful as needed

Dandruff Lotion
Ingredients:
Mix 2 cups of witch hazel and ½ cup of lemon juice
Dab the mixture with a cotton ball on the whole scalp area

Depression
Drink a tea made by boiling 1 tsp of crushed Kava-kava cut root in 8 oz of water

Diabetes
Reduce your weight to a healthy level
Enjoy a daily 80% Salad and Vegetable diet and 30 minutes of exercise
Choose one of the following teas daily -
Drink a tea made by boiling 1 tsp of crushed Pink lady slipper root in 1 cup of water
Drink a tea made by boiling 1 tsp of crushed Adams needle leaves in 1 cup of water
Drink a tea made by boiling 1 tsp of crushed Buckle berry leaves in 1 cup of water
Drink a tea made by boiling 1 tsp of crushed Red root in 1 cup of water

Diarrhea
Grate one ripe apple
Set the pulp aside at room temperature for several hours until darkened and eat

Chew False aloe root for stubborn diarrhea
or
Choose one of the following teas daily -
Drink a tea made by boiling 1 tsp of crushed Alum root in 1 cup of water
Drink a tea made by boiling 1 tsp of crushed Sassafras tap root in 1 cup of water
Drink a tea made by boiling 1 tsp of crushed Weed root in 1 cup of water
Drink a tea made by boiling 1 tsp of crushed Agrimony Herb leaves in 1 cup of water

Disinfectant
Goldenseal leaves washed, crushed and rubbed on cuts, scrapes, boils and acne
Alcohol rubbed on cuts, scrapes, boils and acne

Diuretic
Dried Buchu leaf sprinkled over the food
Cabbage as a salad or side dish
Celery in a salad
Drink a tea made by boiling 1 tbsp of crushed Chickweed leaves in 1 cup of water

Earache
Insert 1 drop of lukewarm (not hot) baby oil gently in the ear (for children)
Insert 2 drops of lukewarm (not hot) olive oil gently in ear
or
A small piece of Black how bark or Mullein leaf (Placed in the outer lobe of the ear)

Energy stimulant
Drink a tea made by boiling 1 tbsp of crushed Ginseng root in 1 cup of water

Eyewash –
Make a tea of 1 tbsp of crushed Allspice bark
Boil it in 1 cup of water
Allow it to cool

Strain and refrigerate for use
(shelf life – up to 5 days)
Gently apply it to the eyes
Gently dry them
(it may be used up to 8 times a day)
Ingredients:
2 tbsp of ground comfrey root
2 tbsp of ground fennel seeds
2 cups of water
2 tsp of crushed goldenseal root
Preparation:
Boil the comfrey root, fennel seeds in the water and simmer
for 3 minutes
Allow to cool
Strain and refrigerate for use (shelf life – 5 days)
Use and wash the eyes up to 8 times a day
or
Cut an onion and hold near the effected eye – the eye will
water (natural eyewash)

Eyesight
Eat raw carrots
Queen Anne lace root cut and eaten in salads

Female problems –
Drink a tea made by boiling 1 tbsp of crushed Black cohosh
root in 1 cup of water

Fever Reducer -
Steep 1 tsp of crushed Willow bark in boiling water for 10
minutes as a tea
Steep 1 tsp of crushed Wood-sorrel leaves in boiling water for
10 minutes as tea
Steep 1 tsp of crushed Peppermint leaves in boiling water for
10 minutes as tea
Steep 1 tsp of crushed Maidenhair leaves in boiling water for
10 minutes as tea
Steep 1 tsp of crushed Cardinal flower leaves in boiling water
for 10 minutes as tea

Place a thick slice of Onion under the feet and leave it there for several hours
(Use a sock to secure it) It will turn black reducing the fever

Fever blister
Apply crushed sumac berries on the fever blister
Steep 1 tsp of crushed Wild geranium leaves in boiling water for 10 minutes as a tea
Place 2 tbsp of crushed Beech Drop Herb leaves in 1 cup of water for 12 hours, strain and use as a mouthwash

Gallstone Eliminator
Drink ½ a cup of apple cider vinegar before breakfast, lunch, dinner and bedtime
Then for 4 days mix and drink ¼ cup of apple cider vinegar and ¼ cup of olive oil
(Do that before breakfast, lunch, dinner and bedtime)
The stones should pass after that

Gas and bloating
Eat ½ tsp of ground Anise seed
Tea made of 1 tsp of crushed Wild ginger root in boiling water for 10 minutes

Goitre
Add 15 grams of Bladder wrack plant leaves in salad

Gum infection
Mix I tsp of crushed Sesame seed in 1 cup of water – swoosh in the mouth first thing in morning

Hay fever or allergies
Eat local Honey

Headache
Scrape ½ tsp of the white inner bark of a Willow Tree (use up to 4 times per day)
(It also serves as a blood thinner)

Heart disease
Oatmeal – good for the cardiovascular system
Hawthorne crushed red berries and flowers used in salads

Heart tonic
Place 1 tsp of cut Lilly of valley root in 1 cup of water for 2 hours, strain and drink
Boil 1 tsp of Celery seeds in 1 cup of water and steep for 15 minutes for tea
Tomatoes

Haemorrhoids or piles
Try a warm bath
Consume 30 grams of dietary fibre and 10 pints of water daily
Stool may be softened by eating Psyllium seed husks
Soothe the affected area by applying witch hazel or aloe vera gel
Eliminate spicy and acidic foods
Add Turnips to a salad daily
A tablespoon of ground sesame seeds boiled in water to reduce it by half
(Drink ¼ cup twice per day)
A poultice formed from ground Evening primrose roots, applied to the affected area

Haemorrhoid salve
Ingredients:
    3 tbsp of honey
    2 tsp of powdered comfrey root
    3 tbsp of aloe-vera gel
    3 tbsp of powdered Evening primrose roots
    3 tbsp of Witch hazel (place bark and leaves in 1 pt of water for 5 hours and strain)

Preparation:
Mix the ingredients in a bowl to make the salve (not the witch hazel)
Apply the witch hazel liquid to the affected area to soothe
Then smear on a thin layer of the salve
Do this 3 times per day and after every bowel movement

Hiccups
Boil 1 tsp of ground Fennel seed in 1 cup of water and steep for 15 minutes for tea
Eat a spoonful of white sugar

Immune stimulator
Garlic - raw
Oregano oil over salad
Shitake mushrooms
Infusion made by placing 1 tbsp of Echinacea cut root in 2 cups of water for 5 hours and straining it for use
(Drink 1 cup in the morning and evening)
Infusion made by placing 1 tbsp of cut Astragalus root in 2 cups of water for 5 hours and straining it for use (Drink 1 cup in the morning and evening)
A tea made by boiling and steeping 1 tsp of ground Ginseng root in 1 cup of water
A tea made by boiling and steeping 1 tsp of ground Wild indigo root in 1 cup of water
A tea made by boiling and steeping 1 tsp of ground Red clover plant in 1 cup of water
A tea made by boiling and steeping 1 tsp of ground Pau Doarco bark in 1 cup of water

Indigestion/Heartburn
Take 1 tbsp of Vinegar before meals or when needed
or
Eat finely cut slices of a Cucumber
or
Drink 1 teaspoon of baking soda mixed in 1 cup of water (Up to 3 times per day)

Inflammation
On the exterior of the body:
Soak the affected part in ice water or cover with an ice pack
Apply ground Passion flower root to the affected area to extract the inflammation
Arnica flowers crushed into a paste and placed on swelling or painful joints
Boswelia cream applied to arthritis areas

Eat pineapple
Grape seeds – ground and eaten for swelling
Drink a tea made by boiling and steeping 1 tsp of ground
Devils claw root in 1 cup of water (Use for arthritis and lower
back pain)
Drink a tea made by boiling and steeping 1 tsp of cut
Marshmallow root in 1 cup of water
Dried and ground Turmeric root – 1 tsp with each meal (for
arthritis and tendonitis)
Finely ground Marigold mixed in a cream and applied to the
affected area
(Sunburn, skin irritation and insect bites)
Drink a tea made by boiling and steeping 1 tsp of cut Ginger
root in 1 cup of water
(Use for arthritis and bursitis)
Infusion of 1 tbsp of Burdock cut root in 1 pt of water for 5
hours, strained and applied to the affected area

Influenza
Mix 2 tsp of Elder Flowers and 2 tsp of peppermint leaves in
1 cup of boiling water
(Drink as a hot tea)

Insomnia
Drink a tea made by boiling and steeping 1 tsp of ground
Catnip leaves in 1 cup of water
Infusion of 1 tbsp of cut Valerian root in 2 cups of water for 5
hours, strain and drink.
(Drink 1 tsp with 4 tbsp of water 40 minutes before bedtime)

Intestinal lining
Drink spinach and greens that are blended into a juice – for
Chlorophyll

Jaundice
Drink a tea made by boiling and steeping 1 tsp of cut Barberry
Root in 1 cup of water.
(Do Not Take During Pregnancy or for more than 1 month)

Kidney – urinary tract infection
A tea made by boiling and steeping 1 tsp of cut Hydrangea root in 1 cup of water
A tea made by boiling and steeping 1 tsp of Duckweed leaves in 1 cup of water

Kidney stones
A tea made by boiling and steeping 1 tsp of cut Burdock root in 1 cup of water
A tea made by boiling and steeping 1 tsp of cut Joe-Pye weed root in 1 cup of water

Laxative
A tea made by boiling and steeping 1 tsp of cut Blue flag root in 1 cup of water
A tea made by boiling and steeping 1 tsp of cut Cascara bark weed root in 1 cup of water
A tea made by boiling and steeping 1 tsp of cut Slippery elm bark in 1 cup of water

Lice
Larkspur seeds ground – rubbed in hair or on the affected area

Liniments
How to prepare and use liniments:
- Mix the ingredients
- Store in a glass bottle for a week
- Shake it well every day before use
- Massage it on the affected area
Liniments used for:
Age Spots
Ingredients:
Red root, Goldenseal root, Burdock root, Yellow Dock root, Blood Root, Red Clover blooms, Sheep Sorrel leaves and Poke berries (1 tbsp of each finely ground)
Mix the ingredients into 16 oz of Isopropyl Alcohol (or Vodka – do not drink)
Shake daily for one week and then strain

Living in Difficult Times

Apply to the affected area (Avoid the eyes, mouth, nostrils and very sensitive areas)
Arthritis, Bruises, Cuts, Fever, Insect bites, Muscle pain, Poison Ivy and Stings
Ingredients:
Mix 1 tbsp of Myrrh gum, 1 tbsp of Goldenseal root powder and 1 ground Capsicum fruit
Mix into 1 cup of Isopropyl Alcohol (or Vodka – do not drink)
Shake daily for one week and then strain
Apply to the affected area (Avoid the eyes, mouth, nostrils and very sensitive areas)
Rheumatism, Arthritis, Bursitis and Muscle cramps
Ingredients:
Mix 1 tbsp of Witch Hazel bark, 1 tbsp of Squaw Vine leaves and 1 Capsicum fruit
Mix into 1 cup of Isopropyl Alcohol (or Vodka – do not drink)
Shake daily for one week and then strain
Apply to the affected area (Avoid the eyes, mouth, nostrils and very sensitive areas)
Skin Diseases, Poison Ivy, Poison Oak, Shingles, Lupus, Psoriasis and Eczema
Ingredients:
Mix ground Black Walnut hulls, Poke berries, ground Witch Hazel bark, ground White Oak bark, Myrrh gum, Jewelweed leaves, ground Blood root and ground Solomon Seal root
(1 tbsp of each)
Mix in 2 cups of Isopropyl Alcohol (or Vodka – do not drink)
Shake daily for one week and then strain
Apply to the affected area (Avoid the eyes, mouth, nostrils and very sensitive areas)
Warts & Corns
Ingredients:
Mix ground Blood root, Jewelweed leaves, Mullein leaves, ground May apple root and ground Black Indian Hemp root
(1 tbsp of each)
Mix in 1 cup of apple cider vinegar
Shake daily for one week and then strain
Apply to the wart or corn (Avoid the eyes, mouth, nostrils and very sensitive areas)
Sprains, bruises, rheumatism, neuralgia

Ingredients:
2 tbsp of red pepper
8 tbsp of lobelia extract
½ tbsp of oil of wormwood
½ tbsp of oil of rosemary
½ tbsp of oil of spearmint
8 oz of Isopropyl Alcohol (or Vodka – do not drink)
Mix and store in a glass bottle for 5 days
Shake and massage on affected area
or
1 ounce of powdered goldenseal root
Mix in 1 cup of alcohol (or Vodka – do not drink) store in a glass bottle for 5 days
Shake and massage on affected area

Lip salve
Ingredients:
½ cup of sesame oil
5 tsp of melted beeswax
4 tbsp of camphor
Flavouring of your choice
Preparation:
Mix and boil the ingredients
Add to a container and stir until it has cooled
Place a lid on the container
Apply to the lips when needed

Liver
Queen Anne's lace root eaten in a salad
A tea made by boiling and steeping 1 tsp of cut Blessed thistle leaf in 1 cup of water
A tea made by boiling and steeping 1 tsp of cut May apple root in 1 cup of water
A tea made by boiling and steeping 1 tsp of cut Milk thistle leaves in 1 cup of water
Mix 1 tbsp of cut White ash tree inner bark in 2 cups of water for 12 hours and strain
(Use 1 tbsp, 3 times per day as a tonic)

Lungs
A tea made by boiling and steeping 1 tsp of cut Golden rod root in 1 cup of water

Measles
A tea made by boiling and steeping 1 tsp of cut Ground ivy leaves in 1 cup of water
A tea made by boiling and steeping 1 tsp of cut Silver maple bark in 1 cup of water

Menstrual or vaginal – yeast infection
Mix 1 sliced Beetroot and 1 tbsp of cut Iron weed root in 1 cup of Vodka
Mix and store in a glass bottle for 5 days and strain
(Use 1 tbsp twice per day)

Memory
Mix 2 tbsp of cut Gingko leaves in 1 cup of Vodka
Mix and store in a glass bottle for 5 days and strain
(Use 1 tbsp per day)
Or eat walnuts and fish

Menstrual cramps
Mix1 tbsp of cut Black cohosh root in 1 cup of Vodka
Mix and store in a glass bottle for 5 days and strain
(Use 1 tsp 3 times per day for up to 4 months)
or
A tea made by boiling and steeping 2 tbsp of cut Blue Cohosh root in 1 cup of water
(Use 1 tbsp 3 times per day)

Migraine
A tea made by boiling and steeping 1 tbsp of cut Bay leaves in 1 cup of water
or
Mix cut 1 tbsp of cut Feverfew fresh leaves in 1 cup of water, for 8 hours and strain

(Use 1 tsp mixed in a glass of water)

Mouthwash and gargle
Mix 1 tbsp of Alder Bark crushed leaves in 1 cup of water for 8 hours and strain
Place in a glass bottle
Mouthwash and gargle
or
Mouthwash with aloe-vera juice to sooth inflamed and bleeding gum
or
Mix 1 tsp of ground cloves and cinnamon in a ¼ cup of warm water
Mouthwash, gargle and do not swallow
or
Mouthwash with witch hazel and chamomile to strengthen the gums

Mouth sores
Chew Wood-sorrel leaves
Chew White oak bark
A tea made by steeping 2 tbsp of cut Wild geranium leaves in 1 cup of water
Mix 1 tbsp of cut Beech Drop Herb in 1 cup of water, for 8 hours and strain
Then mix 1 tsp in a glass of water and mouthwash

Mumps
Drink ½ cup of orange or lemon juice diluted with ½ cup of warm water for a 3 days
When the swelling has subsided, eat fruit only for 4 days
or
Drink Green tea – 3 times per day
A tea made by steeping 1 tbsp of crushed Bay Elderberry flowers in 1 cup of water
(Twice per day)
A tea made by steeping 1 tbsp of cut Cats claw root bark in 1 cup of water
(3 times per day)
or

Peel the pineapple plant stem, crush it and press out the juice
(It contains a substance called Bromelain)
Drink ¼ cup, 3 times per day

Muscle fatigue
Eating the white inside of a watermelon

Muscle pain
Grind Black birch tree twigs and water to a paste and apply
to the affected area
Grind Rhododendron leaves to a paste and apply to the
affected area
Mix 1 tbsp of cut Arnica dried blossoms in 1 cup of water, for
8 hours and strain
(Apply to the muscle pain area)

Muscle cramps
Rub a slice of onion on an exterior muscle cramp area
Eat a banana for potassium that helps muscle cramps
Drink milk for calcium and vitamin D that helps muscle cramps
Get some sunshine for vitamin D that helps muscle cramps

Nausea - vomiting
Drink a mixture of 1 tsp of ginger juice and 1 tsp of onion
juice

Nerves
Mix 1 tbsp of cut True blue skullcap herb in 1 cup of Vodka
Place in a glass bottle and store for 5 days and strain
Use 1 tsp 3 times per day

Nosebleed (Could be a sign of high blood pressure-then treat as such)

or
Remain calm
Gently blow out nose to remove clots
Sit upright
Pinch nose closed halfway down the Nose Bridge and hold for
5 minutes
It should slow or stop the bleeding

Chapter Nine: Information about wild plants and remedies

Pain
Scrape the white inner bark of a Willow Tree – just below the outer skin of the bark
Use ½ tsp up to 4 times per day
(It is a blood thinner)
Mix 3 crushed Magnolia closed flower buds in 2 cups of water for 8 hours and strain
(Use 2 cups per day)
Migraine - Chew a Feverfew leaf (Only do this twice per day)
Drink a tea made by steeping 1 tbsp of cut Wild lettuce leaves in 1 cup of water

Poison ivy, oak or other rashes
The juice of Jewelweed leaves and flowers may be applied to the affected area
Crushed Saw palmetto berries may be applied to the affected area
Kelp may be applied to the affected area

Rheumatism
Crushed Rhododendron leaves may be applied to the affected area

Scars of the skin
Vitamin E may be applied everyday to the affected area over a period of time

Shingles
Take vitamin C
Drink a tea made by boiling and steeping 1 tbsp of cut Olive leaf in 1 cup of water
Go on an 80% fruit and vegetable diet

Sinusitis
Mix 1 tsp of baking soda in 1 cup of warm water
Squirt the solution with a dropper into one nostril at a time
Breathe through your mouth while doing this
Gently blow your nose and repeat the action until you have used the solution

Skin
Chickweed crushed leaves and flowers applied to the affected area
(Used for tumours, insect stings, insect bites and external wounds)
or
Crushed Jewelweed herb applied to the affected area
or
Crushed Wild strawberry leaves used as a skin antiseptic wash, applied to the affected area
Use Avocado to smear on chapped skin

Sleep
Steep 1 tbsp of Rosemary herb in 1 cup of boiling water and drink 40 minutes before sleep
Steep 1 tbsp of Valerian leaf in 1 cup of boiling water, and drink 40 minutes before sleep

Sores or exterior cancer
Apply a ripe mashed banana to an oozing sore
Apply a poultice of fresh Wood sorrel leaves on old sores or ulcers
Apply fresh crushed Plantain leaves on wounds, sores and ulcers
Apply fresh crushed Agrimony leaves on sores
Apply fresh crushed Witch hazel leaves on sores
Apply fresh crushed Marshmallow leaves to draw out abscesses, boils and ulcers
Use the juice from Trout lily leaves, warm it and apply it on sores that won't heal
Grind ripe Oil nut fruit and root to a paste and apply on sores that won't heal
Apply dried powdered Poke root on old sores
Apply dried Comfrey leaves and root on severe sores
Apply ground Passion flower root on sores that have inflammation

Sore throat
Drink a tea made by boiling and steeping 1 tbsp of Agrimony Herb in 1 cup of water

Drink a tea made by boiling and steeping 1 tbsp of Alum Root in 1 cup of water

Stimulant
Eat Bee Pollen

Stomach - upset
A tea made by boiling and steeping 1 tbsp of Thyme leaves in 1 cup of water
Cook 1 tbsp of crushed Kudzu root in a cup of water until it thickens – cool and drink

Stomach ulcers
Mix 1 tsp of ground Liquorice root in 1 cup of warm water (Use only 1 cup first thing in morning)
Mix 1 tsp of ground Slippery Elm root in ¼ cup of hot water and allow cooling for 10 minutes (drink first thing in the morning)
Eat a banana each morning

Mix 1 tbsp of cut Virgins bower root in 1 cup of water for 8 hours and strain
Use 1 tbsp 3 times per day
Mix 1 tsp of ground Marshmallow root in ¼ cup of hot water and allow cooling for 10 minutes - (Drink before going to bed)
Eat small meals every two hours
Go on an 80% fruit and vegetable diet

Stomach upset
Drink 1 tbsp of crushed Peppermint mixed in 1 cup of water

Sunburn
Apply thin cold cucumber slices on the sensitive area

Swelling – external
Apply raw potato slices on the swelling area overnight
Apply Burdock root slices on a swelling area overnight
Apply wet, crushed Alder leaves as a poultice on a swelling area overnight
Place a wet, cool tea bag over a swollen or black eye

Thyroid
Mix 1 tbsp of crushed Bungle weed leaves in 1 cup of water for 8 hours and strain
(Use 1 tbsp 3 times per day)
or
Eat Seaweed and Irish moss – as it is rich in iodine
or
Eat ½ tsp of crushed Poke root per day
or
Mix 1 tbsp of crushed Spice bush bark in 1 cup of water for 8 hours and strain
(Use 1 tbsp 3 times per day)

Throat inflammation
Gargle with 1 tbsp of Sage herb mixed in 1 cup of water
Mix 1 tbsp of Sumac berries in 1 cup of water for 5 minutes, strain and gargle
Chew Wood sorrel leaves
Chew a small piece of Alum root

Tonsillitis
Mix 1 tbsp of crushed Echinacea cut root in 1 cup of water for 8 hours and strain
(Gargle 3 times per day)

Toothache
Cloves – rubbed on the gum around the hurting tooth
Tobacco – rubbed on the gum around the hurting tooth
Mix 1 tbsp of crushed Red oak bark in 1 cup of water for 4 hours and strain
(Swoosh in mouth for the pain and swelling)
Mix 1 tbsp of crushed Blue cohosh root in 1 cup of water for 5 hours and strain
(Swoosh in mouth for the pain and swelling)
Mix1 tbsp of crushed Cucumber tree leaves in 1 cup of water for 4 hours and strain
(Swoosh in mouth for the pain and swelling)
Mix1 tbsp of crushed Pennyroyal leaves in 1 cup of water for 5 hours and strain

(Swoosh in mouth for the pain and swelling)
Larkspur seeds ground and applied to the aching tooth gum

Ulcers – legs and feet
Prevention:
Activate your calf muscles regularly by walking and exercising
Enjoy an 80% fruit and vegetable diet
Sit with your legs raised whenever possible
Avoid sitting with your legs crossed to improve blood circulation
Use support stockings if your doctor or practicing nurse so advises
Massage the legs to improve blood circulation
Reduce alcohol consumption
Other suggestions:
Make a blended drink of the following:
Bananas, pineapple, blueberries, a pinch of cinnamon, cloves and ginger
Simmer a teaspoon of ground yellow root in 1 cup of water and drink as a tea
(Twice per day)
Drink raw cabbage juice or cabbage soup
Eat garlic
Drink Chamomile tea

Urinary infections
A tea made by boiling and steeping 1 tbsp of Wood sorrel leaves in 1 cup of water
Varicose veins
Apply Marshmallow leaves as an emollient on the varicose veins

Warts
Apply a paste of crushed Blood root to the wart every day until it falls off
Apply the white sap of milkweed to a wart every day until it falls off
Apply very ripe banana to a wart, covered with a bandage every day until it falls off

Apply crushed garlic to a wart, covered with a bandage every day until it falls off

Whooping cough
A tea made by boiling 1 tsp of ground Thimbleweed root in 1 cup of water
A tea made by boiling 1 tsp of ground Redbud bark in 1 cup of water

Wound treatment
Bruised Comfrey leaves applied on clean cuts or scrapes and covered with a bandage
Apply Aloe vera juice on external wounds
Apply Melalueka oil on external wounds
Apply Agrimony leaves on external wounds

Worms
Drink a tea made by steeping 3 crushed Black walnut hulls in 1 cup of water
Eat 1 tbsp of Male fern crushed rhizome for Tape worms
Apply a paste of crushed Blood root on ringworms
Apply a paste of ground Black walnut bark on ringworms
Apply a paste of ground Back willow bark on ringworms
Apply a paste of crushed Borage leaf on ringworms

Finding wild plants and herbs Many of the herbs and wild plants are hard to find if one is not experienced in foraging.

It is then necessary to obtain them from a reputable source.

I would like to tell you about John Warner.

John Warner is known as the Herb Man
At the age of six, he accompanied his grandpa into the woods on the Cumberland Plateau of Tennessee.
He was taught the traditional medicinal uses of the trees, weeds, wildflowers and plants.
He learnt to know what they look like, where they grow and what they are good for.

John is a very knowledgeable individual on the uses of nature's herbs.
He is often seen on TV and does herb walks and seminars.

I have walked with him and he has shown me different plants and explained their usages.
I have also acquired his books, CD's and material.
He has a wealth of information for those who wish to enhance their knowledge of Wild Edible and Medicinal Plants.
Many natural herbs may be obtained from him at Warner Natural Herbs.

You may choose to visit him online at -
www.warnerherbs.com

John Warner
7365 Hwy 127 South,
Crossville, TN 38572.
Tel: 1-800-998-2131

Sources of different vitamins, minerals and antioxidants

Proteins
Meat
Fish
Lentils
Beans and legumes
Nuts
Eggs, milk, cheese, yogurt
Spinach, carrots or green beans

Vitamin A
Gooseberries
Corn
Apricots
Melons
Peaches
Cherries
Tomato
Romaine lettuce
Asparagus
Pumpkin
Cayenne red chilli pepper
Garlic bulb
Papaya leaf
Parsley
(The following obtained by foraging)
Alfalfa herb
Burdock root
Dandelion root
Kelp
Capsicum fruit
Red Clover blooms
Red Raspberry leaf
Watercress
Yellow Dock root
Poke root

Vitamin B (Niacin)
(The following obtained by foraging)
Gooseberries
Wild mustard leaves
Wild strawberry

B1 (Thiamine)
Wheat
Corn
Oatmeal
Parsley leaf
Red Raspberry leaf
(The following obtained by foraging)
Wild mustard leaves
Wild strawberry
Capsicum fruit
Dandelion root
Fenugreek seed
Kelp plant

B2 (Riboflavin)
Lamb
Collard greens
Broccoli
(The following obtained by foraging)
Wild strawberry
Alfalfa herb
Burdock root
Dandelion root
Fenugreek seed
Kelp
Parsley leaf
Watercress

B3
Broccoli
Cauliflower

Parsley
Sage
(The following obtained by foraging)
Alfalfa herb
Burdock root
Dandelion root
Fenugreek see
Kelp

B 6

Corn
Tomato
Beef
Tuna
Spinach
Broccoli
Carrots
Cauliflower
Potato
Brown rice
Beta-carotene in vegetables - carrots, pumpkins, and sweet potatoes
(The following obtained by foraging)
Alfalfa herb
Red Clover blooms
Spirulina plant

B12 (B complex)

Chicken
Turkey
Tuna
Parsley leaf
Cayenne red chilli pepper
(The following obtained by foraging)
Alfalfa herb
Kelp
Spirulina plant

Vitamin C

Citrus fruit
Kiwi
Corn
Gooseberries
Melons
Peaches
Blackberries
Blueberries
Green pepper
Green beans
Peas
Carrots
Cauliflower
Bok Choy
Asparagus
Cayenne red chilli pepper
Parsley
Sage
Garlic
(The following obtained by foraging)
Sheep sorrel leaves
Watercress
Alfalfa herb
Burdock root
Dandelion root
Fenugreek seed
Kelp
Capsicum fruit
Spirulina plant
Red Clover blooms
Chickweed
Poke root
Yellow Dock root
Lobelia herb

Vitamin D

Gooseberries
Salmon
Milk

Yogurt
(The following obtained by foraging)
Alfalfa herb
Watercress

Vitamin E
Yellow Squash
Apple
E Oil
Eggs
Avocado
Turnip greens
Cayenne red chilli pepper
Red Raspberry leaf
(The following obtained by foraging)
Alfalfa herb
Dandelion root
Kelp
Watercress

Vitamin G
(The following obtained by foraging)
Alfalfa herb
Capsicum fruit
Dandelion root
Gota Kola herb
Kelp

Vitamin K
(The following obtained by foraging)
    Stinging nettle
    Alfalfa herb
    Plantain root
    Shepherds Purse

Multi-vitamins
(The following obtained by foraging)
    Kelp plant
    Capsicum fruit
    Alfalfa herb
    Spirulina plant
    Burdock root
    Red Clover blooms
    Chickweed
    Watercress
    Fenugreek seed
    Bee Pollen

Selenium
Dietary selenium from cereals, meat, fish, and eggs

Potassium
    Bananas
    Gooseberries
    Corn
    Broccoli
    Cauliflower
    Cucumber
    Chicken
    Beef
    Lamb
    Bok Choy
    (The following obtained by foraging)
    Wild mustard leaves
    Alfalfa herb
    Borage herb

Living in Difficult Times

Parsley leaf
Blue Cohosh root
Chamomile flowers
Kelp
Eyebright herb
Fennel seed
Irish Moss herb
Dandelion root

Calcium

Gooseberries
Broccoli
Brown rice
Milk
Yogurt
Cayenne red chilli pepper
Parsley leaf
(The following obtained by foraging)
Stinging nettle
Wild mustard leaves
Wild strawberry
Alfalfa
Horsetail Grass
Kelp
Dandelion root
Irish moss
Blue Cohosh root

Phosphorus

Gooseberries
Radishes
Leeks
Cayenne red chilli pepper
Garlic
Parsley leaf
(The following obtained by foraging)

Wild mustard leaves
Wild strawberry
Alfalfa herb
Liquorice root
Blue Cohosh root
Capsicum fruit
Chickweed
Dandelion root
Irish moss herb
Kelp

Chromium
Apples

Zink
Oatmeal
Chicken
Beef
Potato
(The following obtained by foraging)
Kelp plant
Marshmallow root

Magnesium
Bananas
Blackberries
Celery
Broccoli
Cauliflower
Green beans
Carrots
Cucumber
(The following obtained by foraging)
Alfalfa herb
Blue Cohosh root
Capsicum fruit
Dandelion root

Living in Difficult Times

Kelp
Mullein
Peppermint leaf
Evening Primrose

Iodine
Fennel seed
Parsley
Kelp plant
(The following obtained by foraging)
Bladder wrack plant
Alfalfa herb
Borage herb
Blue Cohosh root
Chamomile flowers
Eyebright herb
Irish moss herb
Dandelion root
Kelp plant

Chlorine
Leeks

Sulphur
Leeks
Garlic
Fennel seed
(The following obtained by foraging)
Alfalfa herb
Burdock root
Capsicum fruit
Kelp
Eyebright herb
Irish moss herb
Mullein leaf

Chapter Nine: Information about wild plants and remedies

Sodium
Salt
Parsley leaf
Fennel seed
(The following obtained by foraging)
Alfalfa herb
Dandelion root
Dulse plant
Irish moss
Kelp plant
Shepherds Purse

Coenzyme Q10
Fish
Meat

Iron
Beef
Brown rice
Cucumber
Turnip leaves
Cayenne red chilli pepper
(The following obtained by foraging)
Stinging nettle
Yellow dock root
Muscadines
Possum grapes
Wild mustard leaves
Wild strawberry

Copper
(The following obtained by foraging)
Chickweed leaves

Living in Difficult Times

Folate
Eggs
Omega 3 fatty acids – from fish oils and some plant oils such as flaxseed oil
(The following obtained by foraging)
Purslane leaves and stems

Dietary fibre
Gooseberries, plums, berries, bananas, apples
Peas, green beans, soybeans, broccoli, carrots, cauliflower, whole grain foods, nuts and potato skins
(The following obtained by foraging)
Jerusalem artichokes

Lipoic acid
Red meats
Broccoli
Spinach
Yeast

Antioxidants
Vitamin C
Vitamin E
Grape nuts
Coenzyme Q 10
Lipoic acid
Glutathione
Cooked vegetables that are rich in antioxidants -
Artichokes, cabbage, broccoli, asparagus, avocados, beetroot and spinach
Fruits
Cranberries, blueberries, plums, blackberries, raspberries, strawberries, blackcurrants, figs, cherries, guava, oranges, mango, grape juice and pomegranate juice also have significant antioxidants.
Nuts

Chapter Nine: Information about wild plants and remedies

Such as pecans, walnuts, hazelnuts, pistachio, almonds, cashew nuts, macadamia nuts and peanut butter have antioxidants.

The following spices *are high in antioxidants:*

Paprika, garlic, mustard seed, ginger, pepper, chilli powder, coriander, onion, cardamom, clove, cinnamon, turmeric, cumin, turmeric, cumin, parsley, basil, curry powder.

So do typical herbs such as: Sage, thyme, marjoram, tarragon, peppermint, oregano, savoury and basil

A list of Foods providing all the vitamins, minerals and metals needed for nutrition:

A general shopping list:
Vegetables -
Avocado
Asparagus
Bok Choy
Broccoli
Brown rice
Carrots
Cauliflower
Cayenne red chilli pepper
Celery
Cereal
Collard greens
Corn
Cucumber
Garlic bulb
Green pepper
Green beans
Lentils
Leeks
Oatmeal
Oils
Olive oil
Parsley leaf
Peas
Potato
Radishes
Pumpkin
Romaine lettuce
Spinach
Tomato
Turnip greens
Wheat
Yellow Squash

Chapter Nine: Information about wild plants and remedies

Fruit -
Apples
Apricots
Bananas
Blackberries
Blueberries
Citrus fruit
Cherries
Gooseberries
Kiwi
Melons
Peaches

Other -
Fish
Meat
Eggs
Nuts

A general foraging list:
Alfalfa herb
Bee Pollen
Bladder wrack plant
Borage herb,
Blue Cohosh root
Burdock root
Capsicum fruit
Chamomile flowers
Chickweed leaves
Dandelion root
Dock
Evening Primrose
Eyebright herb
Fennel seed
Fenugreek seed
Gota Kola herb
Horsetail Grass herb
Irish moss herb
Kelp plant

Liquorice root
Lobelia herb
Marshmallow root
Mullein leaf
Muscadines
Mustard leaves
Parsley leaf
Peppermint leaf
Plantain root
Poke root
Purslane leaves and stems
Red Clover blooms
Red Raspberry leaf
Sage herb
Sheep sorrel leaves
Shepherds Purse
Spirulina plant
Stinging nettle
Watercress
Wild strawberry
Yellow dock root

Helpful contacts:
Most wild trees, plants or other substances used for relief and ailments are available from suppliers who specialize in foraging, supplies and education.

These are catalogues I have enjoyed reading:
www.herbalhealer.com   www.swansonvitamins.com
870-269-4177   800-437-4148

A Quick reference guide

Living in Difficult Times

Chicken noodle soup
Cabbage soup
Meat broth or bisque
Cream of potato soup

Wild Asparagus
Cattail heart
Green Brier Tendrils
Wild garlic & onions
Cattail stalks
Bamboo shoots
Evening Primrose roots (like beets)
Sochan stems (like celery)
Queen Anne lace roots (like carrots)
Unopened daylily buds (like string beans)
Milkweed flower buds or Wild mustard flower buds (like broccoli)
Wild mushrooms
(Like cucumbers or zucchini in thin slices)
Bamboo
Indian cucumber root
Cattail shoots harvested early

Menu ideas
Sautéed Cactus leaf, Peppers and Corn
Potatoes or their substitutes - raw
Curried Potatoes
Other potato substitute preparations:
Dandelion buds
Dandelion fritters
Milkweed pods
Wild onions
Chanterelle mushroom lasagne
Wild Mushroom Pasta Primavera

Living in Difficult Times

Cheddar cheese
Gouda Cheese
Cottage cheese
Cream cheese

Desserts   175
Yogurt and frozen yogurt
Ice cream
Making gelatine powder
Making Jelly
Custard
Bread pudding
Pancakes
Fruit pie shell
Different fruit pies
Elderberry pie
Apple pie
Cherry pie
Blackberry pie
Blueberry pie
Brownies
Baking a cake
Making icing used for Frosting

Drinks   185
Tea
Coffee
Chocolate -
Beer
Pineapple beer
Cornmeal beer

Snacks   188
Chicken skin rinds
Hard baked bagels broken in pieces, sauced and seasoned
Seeds popped like popcorn
Seeds – sunflower / pumpkin / squash / fruit
Dried grapes for raisons
Dried fruit
Nuts

Living in Difficult Times

286

Asthma
Antibacterial
Antibiotic
Antioxidant
Antiseptic
Anxiety disorders
Appetite builder
Arteries
Arthritis
Athlete's foot
Bee sting
Bleeding
Blood circulation and clots
Blood builder
Blood pressure
Blood cleanser
Blood sugar lowered
Blood thinning
Body builder – natural steroid
Boils
Bones - strengthened
Bowels
Burns
Cancer
Chicken pox
Cholesterol
Cleansing
- Blood
- Arteries
- A new skin
- Stomach and renewed stomach lining
- Kidneys
- Urinary system
- Gallbladder
- Colon
- Lungs
- Nasal
- Ears
- Worm and Parasite cleanse
Colds, flu and Pneumonia

Living in Difficult Times

- Inducing sweating
- Loosening up mucous or phlegm
- Expectorant-
- Constipation
- Cough Drops
- Cough Medicine
- Cough Syrup
Contraceptive
Dandruff Lotion
Depression
Diabetes
Disinfectant
Diuretic
Earache
Energy stimulant
Eyewash
Eyesight
Female problems
Fever Reducer
Fever blister
Gallstone Eliminator
Gas and bloating
Goitre
Gum infection
Hay-fever and allergies
Headaches
Heart disease
Heart tonic
Haemorrhoids or piles
Haemorrhoid Wipe
Hiccups
Whooping cough
Immune stimulator
Indigestion/Heartburn
Inflammation
Influenza
Insomnia
Intestinal lining
Jaundice
Kidney – urinary tract infection

Kidney stones
Laxative
Lice
Liniments
Age Spots & Skin Cancer
Herb Liniment
Rheumatism and cramps
Skin Diseases & Rashes
Warts & Corns
Sprains, bruises, rheumatism, neuralgia
Lip Gloss Salve
Liver
Lungs
Measles
Menstrual or vaginal yeast infection
Menstrual cramps
Migraine
Mouthwash and gargle
Mouth sores
Mumps
Muscle pain
Muscle cramps
Nausea - vomiting
Nerves
Nosebleed
Pain / Headache
Poison ivy, oak or rashes
Prostrate
Rheumatism
Scars of the skin
Shingles
Sinusitis
Skin
Sleep
Sores & cancer
Sore throat
Stimulant
Stomach - upset
Stomach ulcers
Sunburn

Living in Difficult Times

Measurements:

Cooking Measurements
Pinch = Less than 1/8 teaspoon
1 teaspoon = 1/6 fluid ounce
1 Tablespoon = ½ fluid ounce
1 tablespoon = 3 teaspoons
16 tablespoons = 1 cup
2 cups = 1 pint
2 pints = 1 quart
1 cup = 8 fluid ounces
2 cups = 1 pint
2 cups = 16 fluid ounces
1 quart = 2 pints
4 cups = 1 quart
8 cups = ½ gallon
4 quarts = 1 gallon
16 ounces = 1 pound
¼ teaspoon = 1.25 ml
½ tsp = 2.5 ml
1 tsp = 5 ml
1 tablespoon = 15 ml
¼ cup = 60 ml
1/3 cup = 75 ml
½ cup = 125 ml
2/3 cup = 150 ml
¾ cup = 175 ml
1 cup = 250 ml
4 cups = 1 litre

Weight Conversions
1 oz = 25 g
2 oz = 50 g
3 oz = 75 g
4 oz = 100 g
10 oz = 250 g
1 lb = 500 g
1 lb = 16 oz
1½ lb = 750 g
2 lb = 1 kg

Estimated number of cups in 1 lb of ingredients
Almonds – 3½ cups
Dried apples – 3 cups
Dried apricots – 6 cups
Cut bananas – 3 cups
Kidney beans – 1½ cups
Butter – 2 cups
Shredded cabbage – 4 cups
Grated carrots – 3 cups
Grated cheese – 4 cups
Chocolate chips – 3 cups
Cocoa – 4 cups
Ground coffee – 4 cups
Corn meal – 3 cups
Corn starch – 3 cups
Cottage cheese – 2 cups
Cream cheese – 2 cups
Dried currants – 3 cups
Pitted dates – 3 cups
Flour – 4 cups
Corn Flour – 4 cups
Flour, Rice – 3½ cups
Graham Crackers – 6 cups
Honey – 1½ cups
Lentils – 2 cups
Macaroni uncooked – 4 cups
Milk powder – 4 cups
Molasses – 1 cup
Dried peaches – 3 cups
Peanuts – 3 cups
Split peas – 2 cups
Cooked potatoes – 2 cups
Cooked sweet potatoes – 2 cups
Rice – 2 cups
Prunes – 3 cups
Raisons – 3 cups
Shortening – 2 cups
Spaghetti – 4 cups

Granulated sugar – 2 cups
Tomatoes – 2 cups
Vegetable oil – 2 cups
Walnuts – 4 cups

Calculating Celsius and Fahrenheit temperatures:

1 degree Celsius = 33.8 degrees Fahrenheit

350 degrees Fahrenheit = 176.7 degrees Celsius

Other Books that have been published by Ken Wooldridge

The Apocalypse then Glory (written as a novel)
When reading this book, you will have deeper insight into:
- The unfolding drama of the Apocalypse.
- Powerful players and their roles in the end time drama.
- Dangers many will face.
- How you can ensure your salvation and escape.
- Amazing glories that await every true Christian in Heaven.
- Life in the Millennial New Jerusalem.

Understanding the End Times
By reading this book, the following questions will be answered:
What major world events are about to happen?
What is the true world timeline? An amazing new discovery
How will our lives be affected?
How can we prepare ourselves?
How can we ensure our salvation and escape?

24 Doctrines of the Bible
How convenient it is to locate and read all of these Doctrines under one cover.
It is also helpful when they are provided in a way that is easy to understand.
If you want to know what the Bible teaches, it is just the book you need.
It will help you to experience and be able to proclaim Bible truth.

These books with a spiritual accent will help you and those you love
Available at www.amazon.co
Available at www.amazon.com/Kindle-eBooks
and other retailers

www.ingramcontent.com/pod-product-compliance
Lightning Source LLC
Chambersburg PA
CBHW060837280326
41934CB00007B/813